Why Don't You Understand?

Improve Family Communication
with the 4 Thinking Styles

Susie Leonard Weller

illustrated by Elizabeth Wagele

PARENTING PRESS

Seattle | Washington

Acknowledgment

I am particularly grateful for the training I received through Herrmann International about Whole Brain® thinking styles. Whole Brain® is a registered trademark of Herrmann International and is used with written permission thereof. Graphic representations of the HBDI® Herrmann® Brain Dominance Model are used with written permission of Herrmann International.

Printed in the United States of America
Designed by Magrit Baurecht (Core Creative Team)

Library of Congress Cataloging-in-Publication Data

Weller, Susie Leonard.
     Why don't you understand? : improve family communication with the 4 thinking styles / Susie Leonard Weller ; illustrated by Elizabeth Wagele.
       p. cm.
     Includes bibliographical references and index.
     ISBN 978-1-884734-68-7
     1. Parenting. 2. Parent and child. I. Titles.
     HQ755.8.W4325 2009
     649'.1 – dc22

                                                      2009044855

Parenting Press
P.O. Box 75267
Seattle | Washington 98175

To see all of our helpful publications and services for parents, caregivers, and children, go to www.ParentingPress.com.

Dedication

To my birth family, Bill, Virginia, and Thomas Leonard, and to my extended Leonard and Weller families, who teach me what it means to use one's entire brain.

I give special thanks to:

My husband, Mark, who nurtures me to play.

My daughter, Katie, who inspires me to achieve my goals.

My son, Dan, who encourages me to live in the moment.

My writing group: Ruth Hanley Danner, Cindy Hval, and Janet Boehme who patiently critiqued this book.

My God-sisters: Barbara Guzzo, Mary Hartrich, Pat Lewis, Mary Beth O'Neill, Maureen Reid, Judy Ryan, and Libbie Stellas who've nourished me for more than 25 years.

My Loving Presence members: Lois Irwin, Bea Lackaff, Marilyn Trail, Joyce Tucker, and Sylvia Williams who invite me to live fully.

My supportive friends: Maralyn Cale, Kathleen Wallace-Deering, Pat Bannon, Anne Long, Beth Miller, and Marty Burdick who enliven me with new ideas.

My spiritual direction companions: Kathy McFaul, Jane Comerford, Joy Milos, Mary Rathert, Nancy Copeland-Payton, Jessika Satori, and Sharon Thaheld who refresh my soul.

My coaching colleagues: Deanna Davis, Cynthia Hallanger, Lynn Colwell, Karen Wright, Alison Zecha, and Jody Pawell who integrate body, mind, emotions, and spirit.

My students and co-workers through the Community Colleges of Spokane and North Idaho College who help me to apply what I'm learning.

The staff at Parenting Press who were willing to take a risk with a new writer and all of the reviewers who edited this book.

Contents

Preface

Daughter: *Dad, can I go to the basketball game?*
Dad: *Have you done your homework and chores?*
Daughter: *Not yet. I'll do them when I get back.*
Dad: *No, finish your work before you go.*
Daughter: *Mooomm . . . talk to Dad. All my friends are going.*
Mom: *Honey, don't be so hard on her. She'll get her work done.*
Dad: *Okay. But don't forget to put gas in the car!*
Husband, later to his wife: *You're too easy on her. I'm tired of being the bad guy just because I want her to be responsible.*
Wife: *You're too rigid. She's a teenager. Let her have some fun, or she'll rebel.*

How adults relate to each other and parent their children—tough, soft, or in-between—is a result of preferred Whole Brain® thinking styles, the ways in which our brains gather and process information.* We all have *innate preferences* for thinking in one way or another. They're part of who we are. As in the scenario above, we're often irritated when others don't see things from our perspective. *Why Don't You Understand?* explores how different

Brain Discovery

In contrast to your innate preference, thinking in your nondominant style requires 100% more energy to function.

(Source: Research by Dr. Richard Haier of the University of California at Irvine, "Cortical Glucose Metabolic Rate Correlates of Abstract Reasoning and Intelligence, Studied with Positron Emission," *Intelligence,* Volume 12, 1988, pages 199-217)

*Herrmann International originated the concept of Whole Brain® thinking styles. It is their method of describing how we think.

family members think and shares tools to communicate more effectively. The key to improving family communication is to use your entire brain and adapt your thinking style as needed. Your Whole Brain® thinking style can be compared to being right- or left-handed. You use your dominant hand most often because it's easiest. Similarly, your dominant thinking style is your brain's natural preference and requires significantly less energy to operate. It takes less effort to talk with someone who shares your thinking style preference.

Preferences are not good or bad, right or wrong. However, there are *situational consequences*. Not being able to function in a particular style because you don't "do numbers" or "deal with feelings" can severely hinder your ability to relate to others. It can also limit your success in completing everyday tasks because you don't "do filing" or can't "see the big picture."

Our brains are wired uniquely from birth. Even with two caring parents and a healthy pregnancy, no two children are alike. Within the same biological family, children and parents often have distinct thinking style preferences, just as they have unique temperaments. Those differences will continue to evolve and grow throughout life. Style differences can affect the ability of parents to easily bond with their children and vice versa. A "one size fits all" approach might work with pantyhose and tube socks, but doesn't apply to families.

Since the 1960s, brain research has provided a *biological basis* for understanding how we think, act, and parent. Brain research helps answer questions such as:

- How do I think and make decisions?
- Why do I and my family members behave the way we do?
- How can I nurture my children's brain development?

In this book you'll learn how recent brain research can improve *all* of your family relationships. Each chapter will explore new tools and resources to help you get along better with your partner and your children.

CHAPTER ONE

Strengthen Your Parenting with Whole Brain®Thinking

Are you tired of arguing with your partner about who's too tough or soft on the kids? Do your children play "Divide and Conquer" because they know which parent is more lenient? While you're cooking and cleaning, do you resent the other parent relaxing and playing with the kids? Is one parent passive and detached, while the other is screaming with frustration?

Brain Discovery

Many family squabbles are linked to biological differences in how our brains are wired.

(Source: *Whole Brain Business Book* by Ned Herrmann. New York: McGraw Hill, 1996, page 44)

Being a parent is the toughest job you'll ever love! Some days are more enjoyable than others. What works with one person often doesn't apply to another. Most parents have great intentions to provide the best environment for their family, but differences of opinion arise about which is the best way.

Even the recommendations of parenting experts swing from one extreme to another:

- "Hold firm and use logical consequences."
- "Be responsive to your children's emotional needs."
- "Spend time playing with your children, encouraging them to explore new things."
- "Maintain a consistent routine and structure so that children know what to expect."

The reality is all of these admonitions are valid, because there's more than one way to raise your child. In fact, there are four major thinking styles that shape how you parent and all are legitimate and represented in the recommendations above.

Meet the Whole Brain® Thinking Styles

Researchers have discovered that each of the two brain hemispheres is divided by natural fissures. Smaller lobes within the hemispheres create four major divisions of cerebral tissue. You've probably heard of left or right brain thinking. In addition, people use an intellectual or an instinctual approach to how they make decisions.

Ned Herrmann, developer of the Whole Brain® model, describes the brain as being like a house with four rooms. The two upstairs rooms concentrate on problem solving or seeking new solutions. These are called the Logical and Creative thinking styles. The two downstairs rooms focus on handling everyday realities for survival. They are called the Practical and Relational thinking styles. Although parents might enjoy spending time in some rooms more than others, *parents using Whole Brain® thinking can adapt their style to the needs of the moment whenever necessary.*

Logical	Creative
Practical	Relational

The House of Whole Brain® Thinking Styles

Looking from top to bottom in the drawing above, the Logical and Practical styles are left brain. The Creative and Relational styles are right brain.

Looking from side to side, the Logical and Creative styles emphasize intellect. The Practical and Relational styles emphasize instinct.

Both men and women use all four Whole Brain® thinking styles. The examples on page 10 show some characteristics of each style.

A	**Logical Leon/Lakisha**	**D**	**Creative Chris/Chloe**
• Focuses on the facts • Wants a precise reason to do things • Likes to manage money and numbers • Clarifies the bottom line		• Is a risk taker • Blends and weaves new ideas together • Is imaginative and original • Prefers to be spontaneous and flexible when making plans	
B	**Practical Pia/Pedro**	**C**	**Relational Ryan/Rachel**
• Is reliable and gets things done • Likes things to be neat and organized • Prefers step-by-step instructions • Makes detailed plans		• Expresses feelings easily • Is friendly and supportive • Wants to please others and maintain relationships • Values meaningful and intimate conversations	

Adapted from the Whole Brain® model with permission from Herrmann International

A Whole Brain® approach to parenting uses all four thinking styles whenever they're needed. Most parents consistently use only two of the four styles. "Half brain" parenting dismisses the other two styles as invalid or is unaware of them.

Review the dialogue in the Preface with the husband, daughter, and wife. Apply your new knowledge of thinking styles to their argument. Can you guess which styles the dad and mom prefer, respectively? In this case, the dad blends the styles of Logical Leon and Practical Pedro. The mom integrates the qualities of Relational Rachel and Creative Chloe. In other couples, the roles might be reversed or have other combinations.

People of opposite styles are often attracted to each other because diversity leads to a complete brain between them.

Together, opposites create a balanced perspective. Logical Leon and Relational Rachel's daughter would benefit by learning from *all four parenting styles.*

She would learn from the **Logical Parent** how to:
- Be responsible: fix her car
- Achieve her goals: get good grades in school

From the **Practical Parent** she would learn how to:
- Follow through: complete her chores and homework
- Manage her time: balance competing priorities

From the **Relational Parent** she would learn how to:
- Be flexible: have fun at the game *and* do her work
- Negotiate: know how and who to talk to in order to get what she wants

From the **Creative Parent** she would learn how to:
- Take time for fun: appreciate developing new hobbies
- Discover creative solutions: brainstorm mutually satisfying alternatives

Who is that Superhero?

Parents learn to apply the "Three Ps of Whole Brain® Parenting" by:

- *Providing balanced parenting* that includes structure with nurture, as well as play with problem solving.
- *Protecting family members* from constant stress: a stressed brain is overly sensitive to being controlled by emotions rather than higher thinking.
- *Promoting habits* that nurture Whole Brain® creativity and encourage family fun.

What's Your Whole Brain® Thinking Style?

Using Whole Brain® thinking is like looking at a puzzle and discovering how all the pieces fit together. Begin by identifying

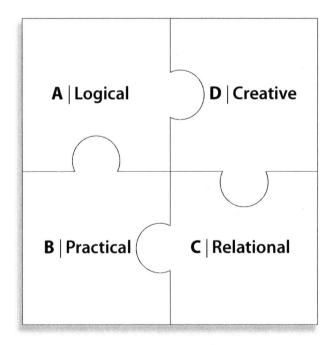

Whole Brain® Thinking Styles Puzzle

Adapted from the Whole Brain® model with permission from Herrmann International

your thinking style and those of your partner, children, friends, and co-workers.

The following informal quiz will provide a quick indication of your thinking style preferences. For a more thorough, validated assessment based on the Whole Brain® model, contact Herrmann International, listed in the Resources section on page 21.

Take a Thinking Style Quiz

After reading each statement, circle the letter of the response that best describes you. There are no right or wrong answers. Choose your preferences, not just what you're good at doing.

1. When you were a child, what did you like to do?

A. Take things apart
B. Organize things
C. Play with others
D. Make up own games

2. What was your favorite subject in school?

A. Math
B. History
C. Drama
D. Art

3. How did you spend your time at school?

A. Focused on getting good grades or other achievements
B. Studied hard and followed the rules
C. Socialized with friends
D. Daydreamed a lot

4. How would your friends describe you when you were in school?

A. Competitive or a natural leader
B. Hard worker
C. Helpful
D. Free Spirit or Rebel

5. *As a child, how did your maintain your bedroom?*

A. Precisely arranged, with any awards prominently displayed
B. Tidy, with clothes put away in drawers and closets
C. Walls decorated with photos and sentimental keepsakes
D. Things bundled in piles on the floor and on top of the desk or dresser

6. *What books do you enjoy reading?*

A. Science and technology-related books
B. Historical novels or how-to guides
C. Romance or travel stories
D. Adventure or fantasy

7. *How do you spend your free time?*

A. Building things
B. Playing cards and collecting things
C. Social activities
D. Watching movies

8. *What kinds of clothes do you like to wear?*

A. Name brand and appropriate to the situation
B. Practical and easy to maintain
C. Comfortable and casual
D. Trendy and unique

9. *What kinds of activities do you like to do on vacation?*

A. Competitive or sports related
B. Planned trips or tours
C. Visit with family and friends
D. Risk taking or adventurous activities

10. *How would you describe your office or work area?*

A. Just what I need, efficiently laid out
B. Filed and categorized
C. Personal and possibly cluttered
D. Stacks and often messy

11. *At work, what kinds of activities do you like to do?*

A. Work with numbers or data
B. Get things done, follow routines
C. Help or teach others
D. Create something new

12. *How do you typically handle a conflict?*

A. Seek to win; focus on facts
B. Restate the rules or past agreements
C. Seek a mutually satisfying solution
D. Create another option

13. *Which do you value more?*

A. Being clear and logical
B. Being reliable and thorough
C. Being warm and friendly
D. Being playful and original

14. *What do others say when they criticize you?*

A. You're too hard-hearted
B. You're in a rut
C. You're too emotional
D. You're too idealistic

15. If you could only use one word to describe yourself, what would you say?

A. I'm realistic
B. I'm practical
C. I'm caring
D. I'm playful

16. How would you describe your cooking style?

A. Measure precisely
B. Follow proven recipes
C. Accommodate to respect others' tastes
D. Improvise recipes

17. How is your home or apartment decorated?

A. Sleek, technical equipment
B. Orderly, with collectibles neatly displayed
C. Family pictures, plants, and comfortable spaces
D. Unique textures, colors, and designs

18. How do you prefer others to communicate with you?

A. Be brief and get to the point
B. Give enough details and step-by-step directions
C. Listen, encourage, and respect my needs
D. Provide an overview and use visual metaphors

19. What do you most consider when you're making a decision?

A. Factual research
B. Practical application
C. Impact on people
D. Innovative solutions

20. What kind of questions do you typically ask?

A. What?
B. When?
C. Who?
D. Why?

Tallying Your Quiz Results

Count the number of each letter circled and write it in the appropriate box below.

As	Bs	Cs	Ds

As: 11 or more = Logical
Bs: 11 or more = Practical
Cs: 11 or more = Relational
Ds: 11 or more = Creative

1. Notice which letter has the *most* descriptions circled.
2. Are there two columns with a similar amount?
3. Which letter has the *least* number of descriptions circled?

What Does Your Quiz Score Mean?

The letter with the *most* descriptions circled is your **dominant thinking style.** You might have the same number of circles under *two* letters, as does about 60% of the population based on research done by Ned Herrmann, using the HBDI® (see page 21). He also found that some 30% have *three* areas of strength. Only 7% have a *single* preference; these people are often experts in their field. The remaining 3% can easily use *all four* thinking styles, and they are usually generalists, rather than specialists.

Notice which letter(s) has the *least* number of descriptions circled. Could this (these) be an area of *avoidance?* Are you able to easily use the skills from this style(s) when needed?

Brain Discovery

"In PET (Positron Emission Tomography) scans, the hemisphere in charge of a particular task—left or right, front or back—glowed more brightly. . . . The scans show that our brains expend differing amounts of energy depending on the task we are performing and whether it matches what our brain does easily."

(Source: *Every Child Has a Thinking Style* by Lanna Nakone. New York: The Berkeley Publishing Group, Penguin Group, 2005, page 23)

Identifying thinking styles is not intended *to label or box anyone into only one style* of thinking. It simply helps people to recognize that there are *biochemical advantages* of working with their innate preferences.

Thinking styles that share the same brain hemisphere—left (A and B) or right brain (C and D)—*find it easier to communicate.* Or they may share an upper hemisphere intellectual emphasis, like Logicals and Creatives (A and D), compared to the lower hemisphere instinctual focus of Practicals and Relationals (B and C). That's why some friends seem to click from the very beginning.

Diagonally opposite thinking styles often *struggle to communicate* with each other. For example, Logicals and Relationals (A and C) are opposites. So, too, are the Practicals and the Creatives (B and D). *Remember, the brain requires 100% more glucose energy to shift your thinking. When you mentally move diagonally to the opposite brain quadrant, it will take more energy and effort.* This explains why we feel exhausted when talking with some people and energized when talking with others.

At times, the top two thinking preferences can create an internal conflict. For example, those who are strong in both the Logical and Relational (A and C) or Practical and Creative (B and D) thinking styles feel pulled in two directions. Their strength is blending contradictory perspectives. Their challenge is feeling drained when reconciling these paradoxes.

Learning about thinking styles has given me a new perspective on family conflicts. Previously, I felt like the odd person out because my husband and children approached life differently than I did. Imagine my surprise when I discovered our thinking styles—especially under stress—were diagonal opposites. No wondered we argued. Now, instead of taking style preferences personally, I accept them as biological variations in how our brains are wired. Respecting thinking styles has helped me to get along better with family members, as well as friends and co-workers. I appreciate our diversity in a deeper way.

Healthy Families
Respect Differences

Healthy families learn how to manage diverse thinking styles in respectful ways. One of the biggest challenges in relationships is feeling threatened by differences. Family members often believe, "If you don't think the way I do, then you're wrong." Those who don't fit the dominant family style are often criticized, instead of appreciated.

Adults are encouraged to be politically correct and value diversity in the marketplace. However, some families have very little tolerance for alternative ways of thinking at home. How many of us have heard our own parents or ourselves insist, "My way or the highway!" If we expect our children to respect diversity, we must model accepting differences at home.

Take the Parenting Challenge

The parenting challenge is this: are Mom and Dad willing to respect each other's style and stop polarizing each other into extreme parenting positions? The more rigid Logical Leon becomes, the more Relational Rachel tries to balance his demands by soothing her daughter's ruffled feelings. When Mom contradicts Dad and supports her daughter's requests, Logical Leon thinks his wife is undermining his authority and values. This further aggravates the situation into a losing battle of who's right or wrong.

Parents who respect diverse ways of thinking teach their children to use all their brains have to offer. *Families are round-the-clock learning labs in which to develop life skills in communicating effectively with others—especially with those who think differently.* Sometimes it's the parents who share similar views, but can't understand their child's perspective. Or, a parent may have a stronger bond with one child because they share the same thinking style, but struggle to effectively communicate with other family members. With practice, every family member can learn to adapt his or her thinking style as needed.

Reminders

- Whole Brain® thinking styles are our natural preferences for how we gather and process information.
- Many family squabbles are linked to these differences in how our brains are wired.
- Family members can learn to better use their brain and upgrade their relationships by using all four thinking styles of the Whole Brain® model.

Using What You've Learned

1. Can you identify the thinking style preferences of your family members?
   - Can your family accurately identify your dominant styles?
   - How does avoiding your least preferred style affect your relationships?

2. How does your thinking style influence your parenting?
   - What are the strengths and challenges of each style?
   - Can you easily use all four thinking styles whenever they are needed?

3. Review a recent argument. How did thinking styles affect the communication?
   - Are the parents' styles so similar that the child's preference wasn't considered?
   - How could thinking in a different way—particularly in your opposite style—reduce the conflict?

Resources

The Creative Brain by Ned Herrmann. Lake Lure, N.C.: The Ned Herrmann Group, 1995. (See www.hbdi.com)

Susie Weller has been certified through Herrmann International to use their assessment for individuals and group profiles. (See www.susieweller.com)

CHAPTER TWO

Support Happier Children with Peaceful Parents

Rachel: *I bought a pair of cute Nike tennis shoes for the baby today.*
Leon: *What? We agreed to stick to our budget. And the baby doesn't need them.*
Rachel: *But they were on sale. I want our baby to look good.*
Leon: *He's not even old enough to walk in them.*
Rachel: *I don't care. I didn't have much growing up and I want our baby to have the best.*
Leon: *You always break our agreements.*
Rachel: *You never listen to what's important to me.*

Within seconds, these new parents are caught in a downward spiral. Neither is hearing the other's need. Whatever happened to living happily ever after?

When Rachel and Leon were dating, she enjoyed how mature and responsible he was. Leon had clear financial goals with a strong commitment to follow through on them. Leon

---

Brain Discovery

Babies have "mirror neurons" in their brains that literally wire them to connect with others—in both positive and negative ways. They copy what they see.

((Source: *Social Intelligence* by Daniel Goleman, Ph.D. New York: Bantam Dell, 2006, page 59)

---

appreciated Rachel's ability to bring out his softer side. They enjoyed exploring their feelings and dreams about the future.

There's a reason Rachel and Leon married. Opposites attract. Now, the very things that used to be so appealing are sources of irritation and arguments. Relational Rachel is a spender. She makes decisions based on her feelings. Logical Leon is a saver who bases decisions on his goals. Remember what you learned in chapter one about *diagonal opposites?* The brain requires 100% more energy to shift thinking to a different part of the brain. It's no surprise Rachel and Leon are struggling to communicate with each other. Not only are these continual arguments ruining their relationship, they're also affecting their baby.

Even babies pick up on the moods of their parents. They'll act fussy when they sense tension. Healthy relationships act like vitamins that strengthen our immune system. Unhealthy relationships are like toxins that make us more vulnerable to stress and drain our energy.

Having a baby changes everything in a relationship. John Gottman's research on "Bringing Baby Home" states that 40-70% of couples experience stress and profound conflict when they become parents. Although this is an exciting transition in their lives, it can also lead to a significant drop in marital satisfaction and escalate previous relationship problems. Half of all divorces happen by the seventh year of marriage.

**Mirror, mirror on the wall – why does my daughter
act like this at the mall?**

So what's the solution? How can separation and divorce be prevented?

*1. Identify your own and your partner's preferred Whole Brain®
thinking style*

Thinking style preferences, like temperament traits, are inborn.
Not accepting someone for who they are can become "irreconcilable differences" leading to separation or divorce. Partners
who share a similar thinking style enjoy more harmony in the
beginning of their relationship. Opposites are more prone to
conflicts. However, when differences are respected, they become
a more balanced couple. Contrasting styles complement each
other, whereas similar styles reinforce only one perspective.

*2. Avoid pushing each other into positions that fuel ongoing
arguments*

Family members who have contrasting thinking styles can get
stuck fighting like cats and dogs. Accept that they're both
beloved pets. Neither one is better than the other. Each thinking style has unique strengths and weaknesses that influence
the relationship.

3. *Listen to the need(s) underlying the behavior*

Each thinking style emphasizes specific needs or wants. Review the following chart and find ways to let your partner know you've heard his or her need and are willing to respect it.

A | Logical	**D | Creative**
• Autonomy	• Freedom
• Clarity	• Play
• Respect	• Inspiration
B | Practical	**C | Relational**
• Stability	• Interdependence
• Security	• Support
• Integrity	• Empathy

Adapted from the Whole Brain® model with permission from Herrmann International

4. *Speak in another's preferred thinking style, rather than more loudly in your own*

When Logicals only focus on the facts and minimize the emotions surrounding them, Relationals feel discounted. The more agitated they become, the more Logicals try to balance the situation by emphasizing a rational response—which only makes things worse. Likewise, Creatives and Practicals antagonize each other by refusing to accept each other's desire to explore options or make timely decisions. Focusing on either/or perspectives escalates the problem. Become better attuned to your family members by adjusting your preferred style and speaking their language.

5. Use non-blaming statements to clearly ask for what you want

One of the biggest causes of family distress is parents who continually complain and criticize each other. *In Seven Principles for Making Marriage Work,* John Gottman writes that there are both perpetual and solvable problems. Sixty-nine percent of conflicts are not solvable. They reflect innate preferences, like thinking styles, and won't easily change. Rather than stay in emotional gridlock, focus on the 31% that can be solved.

6. Express appreciation for one another

Happy couples focus on solving problems and meeting each other's needs. They treat each other like friends who respect each other's differences. They make regular deposits into the other's emotional bank account by expressing appreciation.

The purpose of this book is to help parents not only recognize, but also appreciate their own thinking style—as well as those of their partner and children. How we think shapes the way we relate, parent, and make decisions. Recognizing thinking styles is not another gimmick to manipulate family members to do what you want. It's a tool and a framework for better communication and having more fun as a family.

Let's apply what we've learned about thinking styles to the opening dialogue:

1. What are the clues that help identify each parent's thinking style?
- Rachel makes decisions based on her feelings (Relational).
- Leon focuses on the bottom line of sticking to the budget (Logical).

2. *Which words indicate the conversation is heating up and might polarize each position?*
   - "You *always* break our agreements."
   - "You *never* listen to what's important to me."

3. *What are the need(s) underlying their behavior? (If needed, review the chart on page 26.)*
   - Logicals emphasize *clarity* and *respect* (keep agreements).
   - Relationals emphasize *empathy* and *support* (listen to feelings).

4. *How could each partner speak more clearly in the other's thinking style?*
   - Rachel to Leon: "How much discretionary money can I spend and still stay within our budget?" (She seeks clarification of the Logical's bottom line of maintaining the budget.)
   - Leon to Rachel: "It must have been hard growing up without having much. I can see why you want our baby to have more than you did." (He expresses empathy for the Relational's feelings.)

5. *How could each express what he or she wants in a non-blaming way?*
   - Rachel: "I'd like your *support* (Relational need) to have $25 a week to spend on extras of my choosing."
   - Leon: "I'd like you to *respect* (Logical need) our budget and not buy anything extra unless there's a joint agreement.

6. *What are ways couples can express appreciation for each other?*
   - "Thanks for working this out with me."
   - "I'm glad we're finding ways to meet each other's needs."

Use Whole Brain® Thinking to Reduce Arguments

The top three issues that most couples fight about are money, parenting, and sex. Money is often about power—who makes what decisions. Parenting—especially how children will be disciplined—can surface unresolved issues from childhood and whose family of origin will guide the next generation. Quarrels about sex reveal preferences for how intimacy and one's love language will be expressed. How these conflicts are handled will lead to satisfaction or dissatisfaction in the relationship.

Understanding thinking styles can reduce these typical disagreements. First, we'll look at how a couple handles money. Although the opening dialogue briefly addressed financial concerns, we'll explore it in greater depth and include the perspectives of all four thinking styles. Pay attention in Round One to how each thinking style views the purpose of having money. In Round Two, notice what happens when those needs are not respected.

Money

SITUATION: Jacob and Emily are renting and would like to buy a house

Round One: *Appropriate* Responses

A | Logical Parent

Has clear short- and long-term financial goals
"If we save $100 every pay check we can qualify for the first-time home buyer program in 18 months."

B | Practical Parent

Wants security by making and keeping a budget
"If we write down everything we spend, we'll see where we need to cut back to save the extra $100 each month."

C | Relational Parent

Couples make joint decisions about money and know exactly how much money they have to spend

"Let's talk about how we're doing on our budget."

D | Creative Parent

Each person has some financial independence to spend an agreed-upon amount that is up to his/her discretion

"Even though we're saving for a house, I want some money for fun, too."

In Round Two, notice it's the same situation, but the weakness of each thinking style undermines their relationship.

Round Two: *Exaggerated* Responses

A | Logical Parent

Has short-sighted financial goals. Focuses only on immediate gratification

"I'd rather have a big screen TV than save for a house."

B | Practical Parent

Is excessively money conscious and doesn't balance short- and long-term goals

"We can't go out for my birthday. Remember, we're saving everything for our down payment."

C | Relational Parent

Keeps secrets about how the money is being spent and breaks financial agreements

"I'll work more hours next month and make up the extra I spent this month. I don't have to tell her/him."

D | Creative Parent

Overspends one's personal budget without telling a partner and justifies it

"I make a bigger salary. I should be able to spend more."

Discipline Styles

The second area of conflict is a couple's parenting style—especially how they discipline. Many parents equate the word "discipline" with punishment. In fact, the word discipline comes from the Greek word disciple, meaning "to teach." Parents use a wide range of disciplinary techniques from positive reinforcement to negative consequences. In Round One, parents offer appropriate discipline guidance from their unique perspectives. In Round Two, notice what happens when their strengths become weaknesses and are out of balance.

SITUATION: Three-year-old Sarah throws a tantrum because she wants to eat a cookie just before dinner
Round One: *Appropriate* Responses

A | Logical Parent
Maintains clear limits and ignores the tantrum
"You can have a cookie after dinner."

B | Practical Parent
Keeps the child safe from harming himself, others, or things while having a tantrum
"I'm going to move the coffee table so you don't hurt your head or break anything."

C | Relational Parent
Allows the child to be mad and to express a wide range of feelings
"I understand you're disappointed. I'd be upset, too. You still need to wait for your cookie after dinner."

D | Creative Parent
Explores the underlying needs fueling her behavior and tantrum
"I wonder what Sarah needs right now? Maybe she's hungry, and veggies and dip will tide her over before dinner?"

In Round Two, notice it's the same situation, but the weakness of each thinking style undermines their parenting.

Round Two: *Exaggerated* Responses

A | Logical Parent
Too controlling and punishes any tantrums
"Stop it right now or you won't get any dinner."

B | Practical Parent
Rushes to stop the tantrum before the child is ready to listen
"Cut that out right now."

C | Relational Parent
Feels embarrassed (especially if the tantrum is in public) and gives in
"Here, have a cookie. Just stop crying."

D | Creative Parent
Tries to stop the tantrum by teasing her
"You're acting like a baby—Oh, boo hoo."

Sex—How Intimacy Is Expressed

That confident moment before reality hits . . .

Our Whole Brain® thinking style influences how we express care and affection. We often give what we'd like to receive and assume others enjoy the same type of caring we do. Love signals can be confusing. Some sweet talk in order to receive sex, others have sex in order to receive emotional intimacy. In Round One, look at how each thinking style expresses his or her preferred love language. Round Two demonstrates painful ways couples try to force a loving response.

SITUATION: Alex and Anna are married with two children under five years old. Alex wants to have sex more often than Anna.

Round One: *Appropriate* Responses

A | Logical
Is goal and performance oriented about sex
"Honey, let's get the kids to bed earlier so that we can have sex more often this week."

B | Practical
Wants to feel rested and be intimate in a sensually pleasing environment
"You put the kids to bed and I'll straighten up our bedroom and light a few candles first."

C | Relational
Wants to feel emotionally connected first before becoming physically involved
"Let's snuggle on the couch and I'll give you a massage while we talk about our day."

D | Creative
Wants spontaneity and variety of sexual expression
"How about if we make love in the family room after the movie?"

In Round Two, notice it's the same situation, but the weakness of each thinking style undermines their relationship.

Round Two: *Exaggerated* Responses

A | Logical Parent
Exerts pressure to achieve sexual satisfaction
"You're my wife, I expect you to meet my physical needs."

B | Practical Parent
Makes sex routine or is often not interested
"Don't bother to ask about sex when I'm tired and you haven't helped me with the kids or chores."

C | Relational Parent
Uses sex as emotional blackmail
"You'd better treat me nice or there's no sex for you tonight."

D | Creative Parent
Gets bored more quickly and threatens flirting with others or on the Internet
"If I can't get it from you, I'll have to get it in other ways."

Greater Family Risks Require Higher Family Skills

Brain Discovery

Only 25% of a child's brain is developed at birth; 80% is developed by the time a child is three years old; and 90% by age five. Brains are shaped by experience.

(Source: *www.zerotothree.org/ brainwonders/FAQ-body*)

Children learn about relationships by watching others. They learn to respect or criticize people depending on the modeling they receive. *The biggest predictor of a child's behavior is how the parents get along.* Recent studies in the United States show that 46% of all first marriages end in divorce and 33% of children live in single parent families—the highest in the Western world. One of the challenges for children of separated or divorced parents is that they often see negative ways of handling conflicts.

Although some children are incredibly resilient, we should not minimize the impact of separation and divorce. David Popenoe, from the National Marriage Project, writes, "While marital unhappiness and discord have a broad negative impact on virtually every dimension of their children's well being, so does the fact of going through a divorce. Except in the minority of high conflict marriages (i.e., abuse), it is better for the children if their parents stay together and work out their problems than if they divorce." (*The Top 10 Myths of Divorce*, 2002) Separation or divorce is like a surgery. Although the intent is to prevent additional pain, there are risks and side effects. Children of divorce have a higher risk for experiencing:

- Angry or aggressive behavior
- Grief and depression
- Lower self-esteem
- Impaired academic performance
- Less income and a lower standard of living
- Trouble with intimate relationships in adolescence and adulthood

My parents divorced when I was in college. Even though I was older, I still experienced it as a painful loss. It was even more challenging when my father remarried and moved into my stepmother's home. I longed for the family we used to have and felt disconnected from my roots. I made a commitment to learn from this situation and practice new skills when I married and began raising my children. My hope is that other families will use this book to strengthen their relationships—either to avoid divorce or to get along better in blended families.

The good news is that divorce can be prevented. Adults and children can be taught new ways of communicating and relating that will avoid painful separations. Or, if parents have remarried, families can minimize the strains of step-parenting by practicing new skills. By strengthening a couple's relationship, parents are better able to support the healthy development of their children. When families face greater risks, it's even more important they practice higher skills.

Families provide ongoing practice to learn tolerance, improve communication, and manage differences. Parents using Whole Brain® thinking styles teach their children how to enjoy and act wisely in relationships—especially how to listen, express empathy, cooperate, and work for the common good. Our children are counting on us to increase our abilities to create healthy relationships. In future chapters you'll have more opportunities to explore these skills in greater depth.

In summary, here's another way of explaining how families benefit from using Whole Brain® concepts to nurture relationships.

Benefits of Applying Thinking Styles to Strengthen Your Family Life

A	Logical	D	Creative
• Couples achieve goal of a healthy family • Family members learn from each other • Family enjoys economic advantages of two-parent households	• Family solves problems in innovative ways • Family has more fun together • Family enjoys individual needs being accepted
**B	Practical**	**C	Relational**
• Children receive a secure foundation • Family reduces arguments • Family enjoys a calmer lifestyle	• Family increases satisfaction in relationships • Family avoids messy "ex" relationships • Family enjoys communicating better

Adapted from the Whole Brain® model with permission from Herrmann International

In the next chapter you'll receive more practice in identifying your child's thinking style and using it to effectively teach discipline and other life skills.

Reminders

- Opposites may attract, but couples need to learn how to respect their differences if they are to stay together.
- Separation and divorce can be prevented if parents understand thinking styles and practice appreciation for each other's preferences.
- Children learn about relationships from their parents. The mirror neurons in their brains wire them to connect with others in positive or negative ways—depending on the modeling they receive.

Using What You've Learned

1. What traits first attracted you to your partner?
   - How are your differences causing sparks in your relationship?
   - What supports you to appreciate these traits?
2. What helps you to identify and respond to the need underlying a behavior?
   - How can you let your family members know you respect their need?
   - How would your behavior change if you understood an underlying need?
3. How can you reduce the amount of arguing in your relationships?
   - What are your perpetual conflicts?
   - Which ones are solvable disagreements? How could you spend more energy focusing on what's solvable?

Resources

And Baby Makes Three: A Textbook for the Bringing Baby Home™ Program by John Gottman and Julie Schwartz Gottman. New York: Crown Publishers of Random House, 2007. (See www.gottman.com or BBHonline.org)

National Marriage Project, 2007 report on "The State of Our Union: The Social Health of Marriage in America" from Rutgers University. (See www.marriage.rutgers.edu)

Social Intelligence by Daniel Goleman. New York: Bantam Dell, 2006. (See www.DanielGoleman.info)

CHAPTER THREE

Teach Discipline and Life Skills

Dad: *Please get off the phone and take out the garbage.*

Daughter: *I'll do it later. My friend needs me right now.*

Dad: *You said you'd do it earlier and you didn't. Do it now!*

Daughter: *This is important, the garbage can wait.*

Dad: *You'll be grounded from ever using that phone again if you don't hang up right now!*

What is it about a child that causes well-intentioned parents to lose it? How many of us have made a simple request and watched our responses disintegrate from there? When parents start yelling or giving an unreasonable punishment, they're modeling the very behavior they wanted to eliminate.

Parents are children's most important teachers. When disciplining a child, it's important to reflect on what the child is really learning from the experience. Conversely, children teach parents how to express their love more positively.

Parents use a wide range of disciplinary techniques from positive reinforcement to negative consequences. Each thinking style has particular strengths and weaknesses in how it approaches discipline.

In the opening dialogue, Dad started off fine. He gave his daughter a clear directive and was following up on her behavior. And then he got angry and said something stupid. When pushed, his Logical style became rigid and threatening. Realistically, he's not going to ground her from ever using the phone. His outburst undermined his daughter's respect for his parental authority.

How could he have handled this situation more effectively?

1. *Recognize his daughter's thinking style and approach her differently.*

   Instead of interrupting her on the phone, Dad waits to talk with her.

2. *Identify each other's needs.*

   Dad wants his daughter to have integrity and complete her chores.

   The daughter wants to express empathy to her friend.

3. *Dad speaks in his daughter's Relational style to communicate more effectively to her.*

   "I know your friend needed you and you wanted to support her. I also need to trust you're going to keep your word and do the chores you've promised. Please take out the garbage."

   If his daughter doesn't comply, Dad follows up with a logical consequence using a calm voice:

   "No more phone privileges for the rest of the night until all of your chores are done."

At first it's not going to be easy to speak in another's thinking style. It will probably feel uncomfortable and awkward. That's okay. With practice, it will become easier.

See if you can identify the Whole Brain® thinking styles in the following children.

Five-year-old Connor loves to play with blocks and designs imaginative airplanes. Connor is often lost in his own world, flying his plane on fantastic adventures. If you guessed he has a Creative thinking style, you're right. What were your clues? Words such as: design, imaginative, and adventures help identify his preference. Review the thinking style quiz from chapter one if you need more help to remember the four styles. Now, try putting Creative Connor to bed. Traditional parenting techniques might be appropriate, but they're not his best match. What if you took a blanket and asked Connor, "Wanna go on a magic carpet ride to bed?" By using his Creative thinking style to make everyday tasks fun, you'll get a better response.

What works with Connor may not work for his three-year-old brother, Paul. He's a more structured child who likes to organize all of his blocks by color and shape, and then knock them down. Yes, he's Practical Paul. His parents keep a predictable routine. "Paul, in 10 minutes it will be time to go to bed." He likes advance warnings of what's expected next.

On the other hand, their eight-year-old cousin, Li, can be quite a handful. She's often bossy and likes to argue to get her way. One of her favorite activities is to precisely arrange all of her school awards on her bedroom wall. Did you predict she's Logical Li? Her parents avoid long debates by being firmer about her bedtime. "Li, it's 8 o'clock. Time for bed." They keep directions short and sweet because they know she'll push the limits if they go into long explanations.

Rani, her ten-year-old stepsister, loves to invite friends over to listen to music. They'll talk for hours. She has her friends pictures scattered throughout her room. You're right if you concluded she's Relational Rani. One way of encouraging her to go to bed is by giving her extra one-on-one time. "Rani, as soon as you're ready for bed, chose a book you'd like to read to me." She enjoys Mom or Dad listening to her read.

Now that you've learned to identify your child's thinking style and speak in ways that motivate, let's apply your understanding to other everyday situations.

In the next section, you'll see how parents handle the same troubling situation—when they're calm and when they're stressed.

SITUATION: Abdul, age 4, is misbehaving in the store

Round One: *Appropriate* Responses

A | Logical Parent

States clear choices

"Please walk next to me or you can ride in the cart."

Sets a bottom line

"If you continue to yell in the store, we'll have to leave and you'll lose a privilege."

B | Practical Parent

Rehearses in advance how to behave in the store

"Tell me again what we do when we go shopping together."

Gives step-by-step directions

"First, we walk next to each other. Hold my hand or hold the cart. Second, point to what you want. Third, use an inside voice . . ."

C | Relational Parent

Notices feelings

"I know you're tired. Thanks for being so patient. This is our last stop before we go home."

Responds empathetically with positive attention

"It must be boring to wait while I shop. Think of a game we can play together when we get home."

D | Creative Parent

Distracts by making shopping fun

"I spy a green object. It's about the size of my hand. Can you guess what it is?"

Brainstorms other options
"Hmm, I wonder what we can do while we're waiting in line? Who can stand on one foot?"

Notice in Round Two the parents are more stressed, and they respond inappropriately.

Round Two: *Inappropriate* Responses

A | Logical Parent
Yells
"You'd better stop that right now, or else!"

Threatens
"I'm going to leave without you if you don't come here right now!"

B | Practical Parent
Nags
"How many times do I have to tell you to stop running down the aisle?"

Reinforces helplessness
"If you can't behave, I'll never be able to take you anywhere."

C | Relational Parent
Lays on guilt trips
"I'm so disappointed in you."

Has no boundaries
"Stop that—can't you see you're embarrassing me!"

D | Creative Parent
Is inconsistent
"Stop that whining—here, have a candy bar."

Uses sarcasm
"Oh yeah, keep that up. You really know how to make my day."

Whole brain® parents know how to teach balance to their children.

In a "half brain" world discipline swings from one extreme to another. One parenting camp rigidly emphasizes, "Spare the rod, spoil the child." The other side softens like a marshmallow, always pampering the children's desires.

Parents using the Whole Brain® model *balance structure with nurture, as well as play with problem solving.* They set clear boundaries and follow through on consequences for misbehavior. Guidance is provided in ways that are both responsive to their child's individual needs and appropriate for the situation. Such parents know when to take charge and when to follow their child's lead and needs.

Typically, Logical and Practical parents find it easier to take charge of situations. They give clear guidance about what behavior is acceptable or unacceptable. Children know what to expect from them because of consistent follow-through on consequences.

Relational and Creative parents understand that family relationships are like a dance. There's a time to lead and a time to follow. They compassionately listen to their children's needs and support flexible options. For example, children are asked what type of game they would like to play. They are allowed to be in charge of leading the parents in the game. At other times, parents give the directions and expect children to follow their lead.

Styles Regress Under Stress

Children and other family members have a knack for knowing and pushing on our vulnerable areas. Under stress, we typically resort to using an extreme version of our usual communication style. The Logical parent can cross the line from setting clear and firm boundaries to using threats or giving ultimatums. The Relational parent can be too flexible and give in under pressure. A Creative parent can be inconsistent by not following through on consequences or established routines. And Practical parents can focus too much on getting the task completed and ignore taking the time to enjoy family relationships.

Overdeveloped strengths can become weaknesses. Parents reduce their effectiveness when they only communicate in one way. They limit their options in how to respond and they react without thought. Instead, think before acting and give yourself time to chose an appropriate response.

Communicate in Ways
Your Child Will Hear

Each person's thinking style has a preferred way of speaking and understanding what's been said. Parents know how to adjust their style in order to communicate effectively with all family members. In the following situations, note several possible ways that parents give instructions. Which one would respect your child's thinking style?

SITUATION: Mario, age 2, is learning to use the toilet

A | Logical Learner
State the facts
"Mario, you can't go to preschool until you're out of diapers."

B | Practical Learner
Reward positive behavior
"Mario, you can put a sticker on your chart every time you use the toilet."

C | Relational Learner
Offer positive role modeling
"Mario, watch what Daddy does when he uses the toilet."

D | Creative Learner
Make learning a game
"Mario, when you pee, see if you can aim at this cheerio floating in the toilet."

SITUATION: Jasmine, age 9, is learning to clean her room

A | Logical Learner
Be specific about the bottom line
"Jasmine, your room needs to be cleaned up before you go out to play."

B | Practical Learner
Explains things in detail and sequentially
"Jasmine, you need to do three things to pick up your room. First, make your bed. Second, put your dirty clothes in the hamper. Third, pick up your toys."

C | Relational Learner
Strengthens the relationship
"Jasmine, first pick up your room. Afterwards, we'll play a game together."

D | Creative Learner
Use a game or varied approach
"Jasmine, can you beat the timer and get your room cleaned up before it goes off?"

SITUATION: Michael, age 15, is learning to park a car

A | Logical Learner
Give a bottom-line reason
"We have limited parking. You'll have to know how to parallel park on the street."

B | Practical Learner
Explain what's expected
"Michael, to pass your driving test, practice parallel parking everyday for two weeks."

C | Relational Learner
Encourage often and notice improvement
"Michael, your parallel parking has really improved this week."

D | Creative Learner
Provide a variety of learning strategies
"Michael, imagine you're driving downtown. Visualize all of the steps to parallel park."

Brain Discovery

Thinking styles provide a roadmap to help parents respond more effectively to their children. Identifying and respecting your children's thinking styles helps you to communicate, motivate, and celebrate them exactly for who they are.

(Source: *Every Child Has a Thinking Style* by Lanna Nakone. New York: Berkley Publishing Group, 2005, pages 241-242)

All children are smart. However, they are smart and learn in different ways. Depending on your child's thinking style, some tasks will be easier to learn than others. Katie, my Practical style daughter, naturally likes to straighten her room. Even as a young girl she'd neatly arrange all of her stuffed animals without any prompting. In contrast, the diagonally opposite Creative style struggles to maintain order. Things are often scattered in piles on the floor, rather than in drawers or closets.

Don't assume that your Creative child will want to keep his room the same way your Practical child would. Develop realistic expectations. Creatives will need encouragement to develop innovative strategies for organizing their things that support their thinking style. For example, they might use stacking baskets and hooks so that everything can be seen. Whole brain® parents notice how their children learn best and provide activities that support natural learning preferences.

The next chapter will help you make your home a learning place and support your child's success in school.

Reminders

- Parents using Whole Brain® thinking apply a wide range of discipline techniques. They know when to take charge and when to be responsive to their child's need.
- Positive parenting includes balancing structure (Logical) with nurture (Relational), as well as play (Creative) with problem solving (Practical).
- Thinking styles regress under stress. Avoid overreacting by monitoring the stress level in family members.

Using What You've Learned

1. Notice which thinking style you typically use to discipline your child—your strengths and weaknesses.
   - Try using at least one new guidance tool described in this chapter.
   - Balance taking charge (Logical/Practical parent) with also being responsive to your children's needs (Relational/Creative parent).
2. Review your last interaction with family members.
   - *Structure:* Did you provide clear instruction about what you expected?
   - *Nurture:* Did you encourage any efforts when others did what you wanted?
   - *Play:* Did you recently enjoy spending quality time with this person?
   - *Problem solving:* Did you ask, "I wonder what we can learn from this situation?"
3. Recall a time when you over- or underreacted.
   - What was the trigger? Was there a time of day when you acted more inappropriately?
   - Begin to predict when and why your meltdowns occur.
   - Make a plan to prevent them by focusing on changing one behavior.
   - Rehearse how you'll respond more appropriately the next time this happens.
   - Reinforce new behavior by noticing and encouraging your efforts.

Resources

Growing Up Again by Jean Illsley Clarke and Connie Dawson. Center City, Minn.: Hazelden, 1998.

Love and Limits: Guidance Tools for Creative Parenting by Elizabeth Crary. Seattle, Wash.: Parenting Press, 1994. (See www.ParentingPress.com for additional parenting resources)

Raising Your Spirited Child Workbook by Mary Sheedy Kurcinka. New York: HarperCollins Publishers, 1998.

CHAPTER FOUR

Explore How Your Child Learns Best

Daughter: *Dad, my math is too hard.*
Dad: *What are you working on?*
Daughter: *I'm supposed to do these fractions.*
Dad: *Oh, that's easy. You just find the common denominator and then solve the problem.*
Daughter: *I don't understand a word you just said.*
Dad: *Just listen and I'll explain it again.*
Daughter: *Forget it. I'll ask Mom.*

Ever tried explaining something that seems so simple, but others can't grasp it? Despite our best efforts, they get frustrated and stop trying.

Whole Brain® thinking styles also impact how we process information, that is, how we learn. Recognizing our preferred thinking style(s) helps us to identify which activities are biologically easier for us to learn and do. Given a supportive environment, children can expand their capacity to learn and think in multiple ways, beyond their preferred style.

Effective teachers and parents can explain a new concept in at least four different ways. Like the dad in the opening dia-

Brain Discovery

"When you engage in activities that match your brain's biochemical advantage, you generally expect to attain a higher level of competence in those skills (given sufficient practice), engage in them with a lower expenditure of energy, do them more easily and experience higher levels of fulfillment."

(Source: *Mind Waves: How to Use Less Energy to Avoid Burnouts and Better Connect with Those Around You* by Arlene Taylor. Siloam Springs, Ark.: The Concerned Group, Inc., 2003, pages 123-124)

logue above, we can become stuck by using only one approach. Let's explore how each thinking style prefers to learn math:

A | Logical Learner

Quickly explain how and why fractions are important and relevant to her life.

Dad briefly explains how to do fractions with real-world applications, such as using fractions in measurements and money.

B | Practical Learner

Review each step of the process in an easy-to-follow way.

Dad patiently stops at each stage of the problem. He gives his daughter time to ask questions and checks to see that she understands. Before moving on, he gives her time to practice doing it on her own.

C | Relational Learner

Tell a story about the fractions—either how you learned them, or give each fraction a funny personality.

Dad maintains an even tone even when his daughter gets frustrated and starts to cry. He shares that when he was her age he struggled to learn fractions, too, until his older brother showed him how to equally split a candy bar into thirds.

D | Creative Learner

Use props, visuals, and relevant metaphors to help the child understand how fractions work.

Dad explains how dividing a pizza into fourths will give everyone an equal slice.

Master teachers involve all parts of the brain.

Why Don't You Learn the Way I Do?

Parents often struggle to explain things to a child who learns in a diagonally opposite way. For example, a Practical parent can give too many directions to the Creative learner who prefers an overview.

The other pair of diagonal opposites is the Logical and Relational thinking styles. Logical parents become annoyed when they've explained the task in a clear and precise way but their child still doesn't understand. Instead of switching to another way of teaching, they repeat the directions—only this time more forcefully. When this doesn't work, they blame the child for not trying hard enough.

Frustrated learners shut down when their emotions become escalated. Parents who use multiple methods of teaching stop this negative cycle.

The following chart provides specific tips for how each Whole Brain® thinking style learns best and each one's unique challenges.

A | Logical Learners

- Need a reason to learn the material
- Like facts to be precise
- Want to achieve and be successful

Challenges
- Tune out if things don't relate to their interests
- Like to argue and debate points of view
- Become impatient if they can't learn it quickly
- Are irritated with too many details or stories

B | Practical Learners

- Need time to practice new learning
- Like step-by-step procedures
- Want practical applications
- Enjoy knowing exactly what's expected

Challenges
- Are uncomfortable with changes in assignments
- Become stressed with surprise quizzes
- Dislike feeling rushed to complete tasks
- Feel lost if there aren't enough details

D | Creative Learners

- Need to explore and experiment
- Like to imagine "what if?"
- Want to know how things fit together

Challenges
- Become easily bored
- May need to move in order to learn
- Dislike rules and details
- Struggle to focus and complete projects

C | Relational Learners

- Become restless with too much lecture
- Like a comfortable and safe environment
- Want plenty of encouragement
- Enjoy group learning

Challenges
- Prefer stories about real people
- Find it difficult to do logical analysis
- Need personal attention to perform well
- Want the information to feel meaningful

Adapted from the Whole Brain® model with permission from Herrmann International

It can be quite challenging to respect another's learning style—especially when it's different from yours. When my son, Dan, was in the sixth grade, he was having difficulty writing longer essays. Dan was spending up to two hours to complete a 30-minute assignment. During the summer, his dad and I required him to write for 30 minutes, four days a week, in order to help him become a more proficient writer before entering junior high in the fall.

Dan was struggling to finish his writing task and suggested that he take a break on the trampoline. To be honest, I thought he was procrastinating to avoid doing his work. But he persistently argued his case and I reluctantly agreed to try it—once. I set the timer for ten minutes for writing and then another ten minutes for jumping on the trampoline until he completed his 30 minutes of writing.

After a week of this write-and-jump routine, we noticed that he was writing longer paragraphs with more ease in a shorter amount of time. He's a Creative learner, and the jumping actually helped to focus his attention, as well as release tension. Relaxed brains learn more easily. I'm pleased to report that Dan's currently enrolled in an Advanced Placement English class in high school.

Although many families and schools won't be able to provide trampolines, you can look for ways to respect that some children need movement to learn. Provide regular outlets for moving in and outside of the classroom, and have the child participate in after-school sports activities. Repetitive motions, like playing with clay, squeezing a stress ball, or doodling on paper can be quiet activities that are stimulating without distracting others.

A child may feel stupid in school because he doesn't excel in traditional subjects, such as reading, writing, and arithmetic. Although he plays sports well, excels at making things, or is popular with a wide variety of classmates, these talents aren't recognized on report cards. New research helps parents and teachers appreciate a child's unique learning style. *Encourage children to choose a career that builds on their natural abilities.*

Musicians: Four Unique Expressions

A musician might be a composer, a songwriter, a dramatic performer, or a teacher. Each thinking style emphasizes a different dimension of music.

**A	Logical Musician**	**D	Creative Musician**
• Focuses on achievement • Analyzes music theory of compositions • Likes structured music	• Focuses on individual interpretation • Creates new compositions • Likes to improvise music
**B	Practical Musician**	**C	Relational Musician**
• Focuses on completing the task • Practices diligently; memorizes the music • Performs familiar music exactly the same way	• Focuses on resonating with the audience • Adapts songs to include the audience • Performs music with feeling and moves to it

Adapted from the Whole Brain® model with permission from Herrmann International

Make Your Home a Learning Place

Parent using Whole Brain® thinking provide a wide variety of simple resources to make their home a learning place. Just as you outfit your children with appropriate clothing for every season, make the same level of commitment to equip them with a wide range of learning tools. Notice that the suggestions listed in the column, "Resources that teach," don't have to be expensive or fancy gadgets. You can buy these supplies at the discount and local thrift stores.

Thinking and Learning at Home

Whole Brain® style	Likes to	Learns best when	Resources that teach
A | Logical	• Work with numbers and solve problems • See how things work	• Asking questions, able to do own experiments • Building projects or taking things apart	• Rulers, tape measurers, puzzles, and strategy games • Construction tools and discarded objects that can safely be dismantled
B | Practical	• Read, write, tell stories, and memorize facts • Collect and organize things	• Given enough details and step-by-step directions, seeing and hearing words, such as stories about family history • Arranging data or special belongings in an orderly manner	• Dictionary, word games such as Scrabble®, books on tape, paper and writing supplies • Stacking baskets or shelves to display objects, binders and scrap-booking materials

Thinking and Learning at Home

Thinking style	Likes to	Learns best when	Resources that teach
C | Relational	• Talk, express ideas with others • Help others and share feelings	• Placed in small discussion groups, invited to compare and contrast ideas and interview others • Given time to vent and express how they feel verbally or through poetry and music	• Board games, group projects, and biographical books • Opportunities to volunteer, write in a journal, play musical instruments and CDs, and read inspirational readings
D | Creative	• Design, build, draw, and create things • Wonder about things	• Encouraged to make things, daydream, and use imagination • Supported to observe and experiment with ideas and objects	• Building blocks, Lego® sets, craft supplies, buckets for sand, water, rice, or macaroni, dressup props • Magnifying glasses, microscopes, and fantasy books

Adapted from the Whole Brain® model with permission from Herrmann International

What the thinking styles bring to the table

A family using the Whole Brain® approach honors each member's unique style and contribution. We find ways to respect how each person prefers to think, talk, learn, and do things. We're no longer threatened by differences because we know how to effectively work with them.

Reminders

- Our thinking style impacts how we learn.
- Parents adapt their style as needed to effectively teach their children, practicing how to explain things in four different ways.
- Parents make their home a learning place by providing a wide range of enriching activities and supplies.

Using What You've Learned

1. Choose a skill you want your child to learn.
   - Approach this skill using all of the styles. Which one(s) seems more effective?
   - What would motivate and encourage each child to master new skills?
2. What do you do that comes easily to you? What comes easily to other family members?
   - How do you learn something that's difficult for you?
   - How do you help family members stretch their comfort level when doing a challenging task?
3. Survey your house and notice the kinds of enriching activities and supplies you have. Are all of the thinking styles represented?
   - If you emphasize one thinking style more than another, start gathering inexpensive materials that support the other types of learning.
   - If you're a Practical parent who doesn't like a mess, brace yourself to take the art supplies out of the closet. Select washable materials and swath the area with a drop cloth—an old plastic shower curtain works well.

Resources

Developing Students' Multiple Intelligences by Kirsten Nicholson-Nelson. New York: Scholastic Press, 1998.

Different Brains, Different Learners by Eric Jensen. San Diego, Calif.: The Brain Store, 2000. (See www.thebrainstore.com)

Smart Moves: Why Learning Is Not All in Your Head by Carla Hannaford. Arlington, Vir.: Great Ocean Publishers, 1995. (See www.braingym.org)

CHAPTER FIVE

Speak So Others Will Understand You

Pia: *What would you like to do this weekend?*
Chris: *I don't know. It's too early to think about it.*
Pia: *But if we don't make plans now, we won't find a babysitter.*
Chris: *Can't you be spontaneous for once?*
Pia: *Okay, then YOU take care of getting the babysitter.*

Welcome to the thinking styles wrestling match with Practical Pia and Creative Chris. Both of them express legitimate points —planning in advance and being open to options at the last moment. However, these contrasting needs can quickly lead to an ongoing argument.

So what's the solution? *Don't take the argument personally— different thinking styles are at work.* Creative Chris doesn't like being boxed in by rigid plans. Who knows what the weather will be like by the weekend, or what new possibilities might open up within the next few days? Practical Pia realizes that without child care they won't be able to go out. If they keep arguing their own points of view, they'll remain stuck.

Tips to Improve
Family Communication

How could Pia and Chris rekindle their respect for each other? They can avoid labeling or polarizing each other. The chart below shows how each thinking style prefers to give and receive communication.

1. Accept the way each thinking style uses language.

We each have a preferred way of talking, like our own dialect. Listed below is a chart of common phrases people use when speaking from each thinking style. Do they sound familiar?

A | **Logical**	**D** | **Creative**
• What's the bottom line?	• Think outside the box
• The main objective is . . .	• Look at the big picture
• Fix it	• Humor me
• Who's looking out for number one?	• New, improved, or cutting edge
B | **Practical**	**C** | **Relational**
• Better safe than sorry	• We're a team
• Plan now or pay later	• They're like family
• Do it by the book	• What does this mean?
• We've always done it this way	• Let's talk

Adapted from the Whole Brain® model with permission from Herrmann International

2. Take the initiative to speak in a way you'll be heard.

Speak in another's style by adjusting your own. Review the tips on page 63 to communicate more effectively.

Tips for Communicating with Each Style

A	Logical	D	Creative

A | Logical
- Quickly get to the point
- Provide proof for opinions
- Be precise and accurate
- Allow time for a good debate
- Ask challenging questions
- Demonstrate research and expertise
- Use time wisely and efficiently

D | Creative
- Start with an overview
- Offer the freedom to explore new ideas
- Explain using metaphors and visuals
- Describe the task in a fun or surprising way
- Allow time for creative daydreaming
- Brainstorm possibilities
- Use new and varied approaches to explain

B | Practical
- Stay on track with one topic at a time
- Explain sequentially
- Give clear explanations and instructions
- Provide sufficient details
- Show immediate application
- Minimize any risks or confrontation

C | Relational
- Notice subtle changes in nonverbal language
- Express empathy with a warm tone
- Make time for everyone to discuss the idea
- Respect personal experiences
- Tell stories about real people
- Use informal and friendly language

Get in Tune with Your Family Members

Attunement means that family members understand and know how to meet each other's needs. Families using Whole Brain® thinking have a wider repertoire of possible responses. *What works with one person may not work with another.*

SITUATION: Relational Rachel wants to soothe her children who've been teased at school

Rachel's way of feeling nurtured is having someone validate her feelings. However, she realizes that what works for her doesn't necessarily meet the individual needs of her four children who have diverse thinking styles.

A | *Analytical Allen* prefers being left alone until he's prepared to talk about the teasing. Rachel knows he'll come to her for some problem-solving suggestions when he's ready.

B | *Organized Olivia* appreciates Rachel's help to develop a step-by-step strategy of how to respond the next time she's teased. Olivia relaxes because she has a plan for the future.

C | *Venting Vanessa,* similar to her mom, needs to release all of her feelings first, before she's ready to do any problem solving. Rachel listens without interrupting and later asks Vanessa how she wants to handle the teasing.

D | *Big Picture Ben* needs to view teasing from a larger perspective. It's helpful when his mom explains some children don't know how to express feelings directly and use sarcasm instead. Ben is encouraged to stop taking teasing personally and avoid reacting to it.

Rachel's ability to switch to other modes of communication is like being *multilingual*. She can speak all of the thinking style languages when appropriate. It takes practice to become fluent and at ease with speaking in another way. But it's well worth the effort when it improves the goodness of fit in our significant relationships!

Just as Rachel switches her communication style with her children, she also needs to adjust her style when she's talking with her husband. It's important for partners as well as parents to use Whole Brain® thinking styles.

Create New Relationship Pathways

Maralyn Cale, a life coach from Toronto, Canada, developed the concept of NARN as a way of disengaging from negative brain patterns. When one person starts changing her pattern of behavior, it often causes the other partner to feel out of step. When people continue to practice new ways of interacting, they eventually create a more positive relationship.

The NARN Process

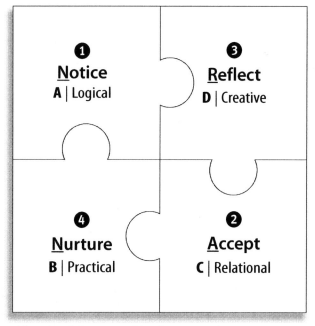

Adapted from the Whole Brain® model with permission from Herrmann International

❶ A | Logical	❸ D | Creative
Notice. Pay attention to the facts. • What are my physical warning signals of stress? • What are my thoughts and layers of my feelings?	*Reflect. Identify the triggers that set off the behavior.* • Ask: "What have I done to make this situation better or worse?" • Reframe how you look at this experience
❹ B | Practical	❷ C | Relational
Nurture. Take action steps to support new behavior. • Avoid repeating old mistakes. • Practice calming down before acting.	*Accept. Ask: "What's difficult to accept about this?"* • Minimize using any defenses to face what is. • Compassionately accept yourself and others without judgment.

Adapted from the Whole Brain® model with permission from Herrmann International

NARN integrates all parts of the brain. You'll notice that steps 1 and 2 and steps 3 and 4 involve moving to the diagonally opposite thinking style. This process uses both sides of the brain to construct new patterns. Each thinking style emphasizes a specific step in the NARN process.

The chart above shows how each thinking style can apply NARN to improve relationships. The goal is to apply all four steps—notice, accept, reflect, and nuture—regardless of your preferred thinking style.

Parents and children who are attuned to each other enjoy being in sync with each other's needs. Every time we get back in tune with one another, we're designing new neural pathways that will make it easier to do it again in the future.

NARN Steps Really Do Work!

While I was writing this chapter I felt stressed to meet an editing deadline. I was grouchy and snarling at my husband, who was preparing to leave on a trip. *To be honest, I didn't use the steps right away.* I was caught up in justifying my negative attitude towards him and not ready to let go and move on. (Remember that key first step about noticing feelings and thoughts!) However, it felt like a lack of integrity to be writing about managing emotions when I wasn't "walking the talk."

I decided to take a break and practice the NARN process. At first, all I could *notice* was how clenched my jaw and arms felt. I acknowledged my mind was in a negative loop that kept rehashing all the things that bothered me. My body felt tense and irritable. I considered stopping and wallowing in my resentments. However, I'd already spent time doing that and it hadn't helped.

After taking a deep, calming breath, I asked myself: "What else am I feeling besides *anger?*" I was feeling *sad* that we hadn't taken any time to enjoy each other before he left on his trip. In addition, I was *fearful* that our frustrations with each other would escalate while he was gone. I *regretted* that I hadn't planned my time better and given a higher priority to spending downtime with my husband.

I continued to take more deep breaths and *accepted each layer of feelings* as being okay—just pieces of information. Then, I *reflected* on what I could learn from this situation. I recognized that I often create unrealistic expectations for myself about what I'm going to accomplish.

Finally, I asked: "How could I best *nurture* myself and my relationship with my husband?" I decided to reprioritize my schedule and agenda to be more realistic. Slow, deep breathing helped to calm my body, but I also needed to *add a positive feeling,* such as appreciation. I *changed my focus* (a calming strategy) from what annoyed me to what I most appreciated about my husband. I remembered all the ways he'd been supportive.

Brain Discovery

In deep meditative states, brain waves shift from the usual patterns of one hemisphere dominant over another to a balanced state of integrating the entire brain. Each time the neural structure changes, positive changes in mental and emotional health occur.
(Source: *Thresholds of the Mind* by Bill Harris. Beaverton, Ore.: Centerpointe Press, 2002, pages 140 & 151. See www.centerpointe.com)

I waited until I noticed *a shift—both a softening in my body as well as in my attitude,* before I called my husband long distance to apologize for my previous tone. The amazing part is that I could tell by his voice that his attitude had changed too—even before I apologized. Soothing my body, mind, and feelings literally created a shift that calmed both of us!

The more we practice the NARN process, the easier it becomes. Our choices create habits—healthy or destructive. Professionals in the field of alcohol and drug abuse recovery have discovered that it takes a minimum of twenty-one days to establish or break a habit. The initial few days and weeks will always be the toughest, because we're laying down new neural wiring, like clearing a path in a dense forest. Although it's slow going at first, with repeated efforts the new path will become a well-trodden route.

Successfully Manage Family Differences

Families are life's learning labs to polish our social and emotional skills. We don't learn how to successfully manage conflicts without opportunities to rehearse and make mistakes within a safe environment. The more adults practice these skills, the better they can model them to their children and use them when they're stressed.

People will always have on-going differences around issues of style—particularly inborn preferences such as thinking

Logical Leon and Relational Rhonda have different expectations.

styles. For example, Practical Pia prefers to have consistent routines, whereas Creative Chris enjoys being flexible and spontaneous.

Despite many attempts to change each other's style, Pia is not going to be able to turn her husband into a Practical Pedro. Rather than wasting her energy on trying to change perpetual differences, Pia's better off finding ways their preferences can co-exist. This may include taking turns of who's in charge of organizing household chores and accepting the others' style of how and when tasks are completed.

Likewise, Logical Leon is wasting his energy using his analytical skills trying to persuade his daughter, Relational Rhonda, to change her ways. He'd have more impact if he appealed to her heart. And Relational Rhonda needs to learn to use her feelings appropriately instead of trying to manipulate her dad.

Relational parents often need to vent their feelings before they're ready to problem solve with a Logical child or partner. First, call a friend and release your emotions to her or him, or write them in your journal. Clarify your bottom line of what you really want to say. Then, speak clearly and firmly to your Logical family members.

Although there need to be some accommodations, our style is an essential part of us. Choose your battles. Focus on solving the conflicts that are solvable. Practice the NARN steps to create healthier ways of communicating.

Reminders

- Speak in a way you will be heard.
- Families increase their attunement with family members when they practice talking in the same thinking style as their loved one.
- Use NARN (Notice, Accept, Reflect, and Nurture) to integrate all parts of the brain and create new patterns of relating.

Using What You've Learned

1. Remember a limitation that you've accepted about yourself.
   - What helped you to accept that this is who you are?
   - Practice using these same skills to accept other family members' limitations and natural thinking styles.
   - Work with who they are, rather than trying to change them. For example, Creatives like variety and spontaneity. Rather than expect them to commit to a specific, detailed plan in advance, just ask them to reserve the date and time and be surprised.
2. Review a recent conflict to evaluate your ability to manage differences.
   - What did you do that made the communication worse?
   - What helped to resolve or manage the tension?
   - When there are diagonal thinking styles, practice speaking in the other's style.

3. How could using the NARN process improve your relationships?
   - What do you *Notice* about your thoughts, feelings, and choices?
   - What needs to be *Accepted?*
   - How could you *Reflect* by reframing what's happened?
   - What practical steps could you take to *Nurture* yourself and your relationships?

Resources

7 Principles for Making Marriage Work by John Gottman. New York: Three Rivers Press of Random House, 1999. (See www.gottman.com)

Being Here Now: Living Gently and Powerfully No Matter What by Maralyn Cale. E-booklet from her web site: www.lifecyclecoaching.com, 2007.

Conscious Loving: The Journey to Co-Commitment by Gay and Kathryn Hendricks. New York: Bantam Books, 1992. (See www.hendricks.com)

CHAPTER SIX

Make Decisions to Strengthen Your Relationships

Wife: *Why can't you just listen to my feelings?*
Husband: *I do. But you keep complaining about the same things over and over.*
Wife: *You never appreciate what I do for this family.*
Husband: *Well, I don't feel appreciated either.*
Wife: *We used to have fun together.*
Husband: *Ever since we've had kids you never have energy for me.*
Wife: *Maybe if you'd help out more, I'd have more energy.*

Despite our best efforts to be balanced, we're not perfect parents. We make mistakes, have bad days, say and do things we regret. The difference is that parents using Whole Brain® concepts are committed to strengthening their relationships by expanding their thinking styles.

One of the biggest challenges in raising children is managing behavior—our own, as well as others'. *Behavior can be changed.* Our responses are shaped both by our biology—our thinking style preferences and how we've been nurtured—our environment.

Children's and adults' brains are literally shaped by experience. Synapses, or brain connections, grow when an experience is repeated. Strong emotions impact learning and determine what becomes stored in memory. Repeated patterns of response become a well-traveled highway. Later in life, the brain is hard-wired to follow these established pathways.

In the opening dialogue, the parents are stuck in old patterns of criticizing and blaming each other. John Gottman writes in *Ten Lessons to Transform Your Marriage* that he can predict with a 90% accuracy rate whether a married couple will stay together or eventually divorce. How? He observes couples when they're arguing and monitors their style of interaction as well as their physiological responses.

Happily married couples *give each other at least five positive remarks for each negative comment.* In contrast, couples at risk for divorce offer less than one positive remark for every negative comment. Their interactions are a downward spiral of criticisms, complaints, blaming, defensiveness, contempt, or withdrawing from the conversation.

Children learn how to behave from their parents. Their brains are particularly sensitive to stress. Kids copy what they see. Have you noticed two children playing, one bumping into the other? One child immediately reacts by hitting back. He's super-sensitive and reacts to any perceived threat to his well-being, even if it wasn't intentional. The other child whose brain isn't so heavily wired for survival, shrugs off the event as an accident. He easily uses his problem-solving brain to sort out the incident and to let it go.

The emotional layer of the brain decides if an event is a threat or not. Any perceived threat causes it to send chemical messengers to the survival brain to protect and defend itself—regardless of whether the danger is real or not. Once the stress chemicals start flooding the body, it typically takes 20 minutes to settle down. As a result, we need to learn how to acknowledge, soothe, and manage our emotions. *Time-outs aren't just for children.* They give everyone a chance to calm down long enough to stop and consider other options.

Whole brain® families quickly use repair moves to interrupt patterns of negative interactions. They know how to recognize both *verbal and nonverbal attempts* to reconnect in positive ways.

Repair Moves that Strengthen Relationships

A | Logical	**D | Creative**
• Acknowledge what's happening • Soften facial expressions • Calmly ask for clarification	• Ask a question • Turn physically towards the other • Use humor appropriately to lighten the mood
B | Practical	**C | Relational**
• Explain without blame • Relax tense muscles • Sit down and listen attentively	• Express empathy and support • Give a hug or gesture of physical connection • Use a gentle tone of voice

Adapted from the Whole Brain® model with permission from Herrmann International

Instead of ignoring or being hostile toward attempts to repair a relationship, learn to respond in positive ways. Some family members need more help to change old patterns of relating. With practice, new pathways can be created in the brain and in the heart. The quickest way to shift emotional gears is to focus on what you appreciate and what you're thankful for. There will be some grinding as you disengage from concentrating on your frustrations. Hang in there and switch your attention until you notice positive feelings emerging.

Whenever I'm really upset, I take a walk down the street. At first, I silently whine how terrible this person or situation is. But when I tag my favorite tree, I commit to changing my thoughts before I return home. I start thinking what I'm grateful for or how I appreciate this person for surfacing areas for my growth and healing. To be honest, sometimes I'm not ready to let go of my complaints. I need to walk farther and vent a while longer. When I'm done, I re-tag my tree to signify my intention to create healthy thoughts and feelings. My spirit is lighter on the way home.

Researchers from the HeartMath Institute have discovered that there are actually *more nerves going from the heart to the brain* than from the brain to the heart. The heart communicates information to the brain and the rest of the body through various pathways: our nervous system, hormones and neurotransmitters, blood pressure waves, and electromagnetic fields.

Whenever two people have an encounter, there's an exchange of energy that either creates *resonance* (coherent heart patterns) or *dissonance* (noncoherent heart patterns). When people are irritated with each other, their frustration magnifies and escalates the situation. However, if one person maintains calm, eventually it soothes the person who is angry to regain control of his or her feelings. Or, at the very least, the centered person doesn't provoke any further aggravation of the problem.

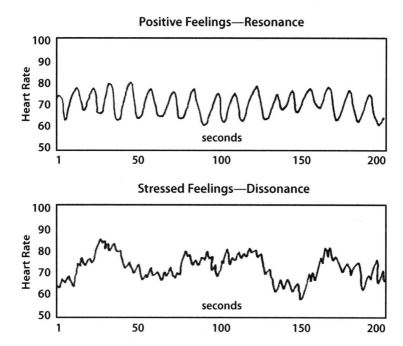

We're often engaged in a neural tug-of-war with our family members. Ultimately, we both win when we do whatever is necessary to remain calm, even when others are upset.

Whole Brain® Decision-Making Uses Your Head and Your Heart

Similar to the NARN process, another tool for strengthening relationships is using the Whole Brain® method for making decisions. It's hard enough to make my own choices, but it becomes even more complicated when there are additional people. Those living in blended families often struggle to accommodate the needs of all the family members and ex-partners.

Brain researchers at Herrmann International have discovered a four-step process for making decisions that involves all thinking styles, in a specific order. This criss-cross sequence stretches everyone's ability to apply all four thinking styles.

Four-Step Process for Making Decisions

1. Gather the *facts*. (**A** Logical)
2. Consider *who* will be most affected. (**C** Relational)
3. *Brainstorm* other possible options. (**D** Creative)
4. Implement a specific *plan*. (**B** Practical)

You'll notice that steps one and two and steps three and four involve moving to the diagonally opposite thinking style. The Whole Brain® method for making decisions intentionally balances both sides of the brain with contrasting points of view.

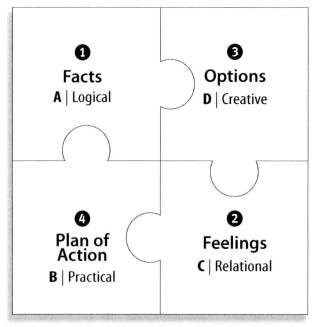

❶
Facts
A | Logical

❸
Options
D | Creative

❹
Plan of Action
B | Practical

❷
Feelings
C | Relational

Adapted from the Whole Brain® model with permission from Herrmann International

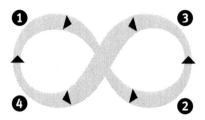

Whole Brain® Walk-around © Herrmann International. Used with permission.

Should Juan get a pet?

Think of the decision-making process as being like the infinity symbol for integrating the entire brain. When implementing a plan (step 4), new considerations will emerge. As a result, you will need to recycle through the process again starting at step 1. What may have sounded like a good idea in theory may not work so well in practice. Additional information may impact people in unexpected ways. Other possibilities invite more exploration. You will probably need to revise your plan. Remain open to learning from experience, and repeat the steps of the decision-making process as often as necessary.

Let's use the Whole Brain® decision-making process in two situations. We'll start with the easiest one first.

SITUATION: Should our family get a puppy?

1. Begin with the facts that **Logicals (A)** contribute to the decision.
   - Is anyone allergic to dogs?
   - What are the initial and ongoing costs of caring for a dog?
   - What type of breed is good around children and will fit our lifestyle?

- Would it be too small or large? High or low maintenance? Inside or outside dog?
2. Second, move to the diagonally opposite corner to consider a **Relational (C)** perspective.
   - Would you like having a puppy around the house?
   - Who would be the main caretaker? Would all of the family members enjoy having a dog and care for it?
   - If you have other pets, how will this puppy get along with them?
3. Shift to the **Creative (D)** corner to brainstorm other possibilities you haven't previously considered.
   - What would your puppy do when family members are gone during the day at school and work?
   - Who would care for the dog when you're away from home?
   - Would you be willing to do a trial run by caring for a friend's dog first?
   - Are there other ways to enjoy being around dogs without having to own one?
4. Your final move is to the **Practical (B)** perspective (another diagonally opposite corner) to make a plan to implement your final decision.
   - Decide if you're going to get a puppy.
   - If yes, when and where will you get it? Pet store? Animal shelter? Friend?
   - What supplies or other preparations are needed? Fencing the yard? Shots and licensing?

When new facts surface, quickly repeat all of the above steps. Use this method to update your decision-making process and plan of action as needed.

Now let's apply these skills to a more challenging situation.

SITUATION: How will step-families share children during the winter holidays?

❶ A | Logical	❸ D | Creative
Start here, then move diagonally to lower right (C). • Clarify what the parenting plan says about holidays. • Prioritize the top visitation and vacation activity requests. • Evaluate the pros and cons of various options.	• Brainstorm lots of options until there are enough solutions to meet everyone's needs. • Blend different needs and interests together to experiment with new possibilities. • Allow unstructured time during the vacation for spontaneous visits and activities. *Now move diagonally to the lower left (B).*
❹ B | Practical	❷ C | Relational
• Make a plan that respects the parenting requirements and visitation schedule. • Decide enough details in advance to be able to make advance reservations and invite others. • Delegate tasks so everything gets done. *End here. Return to ❶ if you need to revise your plan.*	• Respect everyone's visitation preferences. • Listen empathetically to hear the key interests and needs of family members. • Make decisions together as an extended family. The adults put the needs of the children above their own frustrations with an ex-partner. *Now move vertically to the upper right (D).*

Adapted from the Whole Brain® model with permission from Herrmann International

During emotionally intense times, such as the holidays, it's even more important to avoid making half brain choices. No one wins when children are put in the middle of custody battles. Remember to use repair moves to reduce tense interactions.

Are Both Parents on the Same Page?

When making a decision, how do you get both parents to be on the same page? It's frustrating to give children guidance when another parent or step-parent is giving them a different instruction. It's also confusing for children when they receive mixed messages. Parents become aggravated when they feel undermined by other adults.

So, what's the solution?

Whenever possible, meet privately with the other parent to explore coming to a mutual agreement. Rather than argue about who's right or wrong, focus on the end result you both want. Review the situation below. How could parents use their knowledge of thinking styles to give Leah a consistent message?

SITUATION: Leah, age 15, isn't doing well in school

Leah wants to go out with her friends even though her grades are poor. Her parents are divorced. Her mom has primary custody, but Leah lives with her dad on weekends. Mom and Dad are meeting for coffee to talk about Leah.

Mom: *I received Leah's progress report. She's getting Cs and Ds in her classes.*

Dad: *What do you think we should do?*

Mom: *I want you to ground her on the weekends until her grades improve.*

Dad: *Yeah, make me the bad guy. She's a teenager who needs a break on the weekends.*

Mom: *Don't you care about her grades?*

Dad: *Yes, but I don't think grounding her is going to work.*

The conversation starts off well enough. The mom objectively states her concern, but from there the talk goes downhill fast. What could these parents do differently?

Leah's parents apply the Whole Brain® model to help them decide what to do.

1. Logical (A)
Agree upon common goals

- Support Leah's academic success
- Both parents give her the same message about the importance of school

2. Relational (C)
Commit to speak with one voice, rather than undermine each other

- Both parents agree to attend a parent/teacher conference to obtain more information
- Leah will be required at both houses to complete her homework before going out with friends
- They discuss possible consequences if Leah doesn't increase her academic efforts—like losing the privilege of her cell phone

3. Creative (D)
Explore additional options to encourage Leah and to provide consequences if she doesn't comply

- After talking with the teacher and Leah, her parents agree she'll receive tutoring after school
- Her parents brainstorm ways to reinforce Leah's success. They will offer incentives to improve her behavior—such as hosting a pizza party for her friends

4. Practical (B)
Make a plan to communicate more often about Leah's progress in school

- The parents will ask her teacher to e-mail both of them about Leah's academic performance

• Each parent agrees to update the other if Leah has made enough improvement to gain privileges, or if she should lose them.

But what happens if one parent is following through and the other one isn't?

1. *Agree to disagree.* Be clear what the house rules are in your home or when a specific adult is in charge.
2. *Ask and let go.* Make a clear request to the other adult to respect your position. However, unless it's a question of health and safety, let go of issues you can't control. Make a plan of how you will enforce in your home what's important to you, even if you don't receive support from the other parent.
3. *If you fear your child's health and safety are at risk, then you must make other choices.* If possible, talk first with the other parent about your concerns. If that doesn't work, get outside help. Additional resources include the school counselor, your doctor, and if necessary, Child Protective Services.
4. *Trust that your child will adjust.* Your daughter or son will learn which behaviors are acceptable in each house. Ignore complaints about the other parent—"Dad [Mom] lets me do it." Focus on maintaining your house rules.

Most arguments about what a child should do or not do are issues of preference rather than safety. Direct your attention to what you have control over and yield on what you don't. Concentrate on meeting the child's needs instead of debating how you'll get there.

Meeting Children's (and Adults') Basic Needs

Children have four basic needs: attention, stability, excitement, and power. Each thinking style excels in addressing one of these needs. In the following chart, examine the strengths (+) and weaknesses (-) of each style.

A	**Logical**	**D**	**Creative**
Power		*Excitement*	
(+) Self-control and competency		(+) Active stimulation	
(-) Misuse of power		(-) Over- or passive stimulation	
B	**Practical**	**C**	**Relational**
Stability		*Attention*	
(+) Consistency and predictability		(+) Encouragement and support	
(-) Inability to cope with change		(-) Dependency on external rewards	

Adapted from the Whole Brain® model with permission from Herrmann International

Children love attention. When they can't receive it in positive ways, they do negative things to get attention rather than be ignored.

Relational (C) parents can reduce a child's acting out by noticing their child's constructive efforts for attention and offering encouragement. The flip side is when children become dependent on others for their self-esteem. They behave well only if they're receiving praise and rewards.

Practical (B) parents work hard to keep children healthy with good food, shelter, clothing, sleep, and hygiene. Children can count on regular routines. Their challenge is adapting to unexpected changes in plans or expectations.

Creative (D) parents love variety and playing games. At times they over-stimulate children by doing too many things. Or they under-stimulate them by allowing them to engage in too many passive activities, such as watching too much TV or video games.

Logical (A) parents recognize everyone wants to have choices and feel in control over his or her life. In the extreme, children misuse their power by bullying others or acting in revengeful ways to get what they want. The reverse is when they feel overly controlled and react by acting passive or helpless. Statements like "I can't" and "You do it" can be ways of manipulating power.

Parents identify the needs behind their children's behavior (and their own) by noticing how they feel and react to specific behaviors. For example, when a child wants attention for a new accomplishment—"Look at me and what I can do!"—parents are happy to encourage such efforts. However, when a child is constantly demanding attention, parents feel annoyed. Being irritated is a clue they need to help their child feel good about her own achievements rather than always seeking others' approval.

Likewise, it's appropriate when children want power to make their own decisions. If parents become angry, it's usually because the situation has escalated into a power struggle. At that point, it's time to let go of trying to control another's behavior and allow natural consequences to be the teacher. All people want to feel love and support. However, we express it in different ways. Sometimes there's a mismatch between the giver and receiver. We often give what we most want to receive. For example, have you ever worked hard to clean the house and fix a nice dinner, but no one expressed appreciation? They may have an alternative love language. I enjoy talking as a way of connecting but my husband prefers acts of service, such as a massage. So, we talk about our day while I'm rubbing his feet.

Review the chart on page 88 to see how your family members prefer to show and receive care.

Relationships need ongoing nurturing, as well as repair moves when we make mistakes. Rather than argue about irritating behavior, discover the essential need and find ways to meet it. Respecting your family members' love languages will help you be more successful in showing your support.

Reminders

- Practice repair moves by focusing on giving at least five positive remarks for every negative one.
- Use Whole Brain® methods to integrate your head and heart when making decisions.
- Get on the same page as your partner by listening to the needs underlying behavior and establish common goals.

Expressions of Love

A	Logical	D	Creative

A | Logical

Shows love by:
- Solving problems
- Fixing things
- Working on a project together

Likes to receive:
- Respect for their opinions
- Honest and direct feedback
- Admiration for doing a good job

D | Creative

Shows love by:
- Being flexible and adapting to other's plans
- Finding humor in the situation
- Inviting others to do something exciting

Likes to receive:
- Consideration of their ideas
- Invitations to do something spontaneous
- Surprises that are unexpected and unique

B | Practical

Shows love by:
- Giving time and acts of service
- Planning a favorite activity
- Cleaning and organizing

Likes to receive:
- Practical support with daily activities
- Enough details to feel secure
- Offers to help out without being asked

C | Relational

Shows love by:
- Verbally expressing support
- Being a good listener
- Giving hugs or other touches

Likes to receive:
- Empathetic support
- Meaningful conversations
- Appreciation—both verbal and written

Adapted from the Whole Brain® model with permission from Herrmann International

Using What You've Learned

1. Learn to shift emotional gears more easily.
   * When you're upset, take a moment to focus on what you're thankful for.
   * Keep remembering what you appreciate until you notice a shift in your mood.
2. Evaluate a recent decision.
   * Did you use all four Whole Brain® thinking styles?
   * Which styles do you tend to over- or underemphasize?
   * How could you use the Whole Brain® model to improve your choices when making decisions?
3. Respect your family members' preferred love languages.
   * Identify your own and each family member's love language.
   * Choose one way of showing love in each of their preferred styles.

Resources

10 Lessons to Transform Your Marriage by John Gottman. New York: Crown Publishing, Random House, 2006. (see www.Gottman.com)

The Five Love Languages of Children by Gary Chapman and Ross Campbell. Chicago: Northfield Publishing, 1997. (see www.fivelovelanguages.com)

The HeartMath Solution: The Institute of HeartMath's Revolutionary Program for Engaging the Power of the Heart by Doc Childre and Howard Martin. New York: HarperCollins, 1999. (see www.heartmath.org)

CHAPTER SEVEN

Respect How Different Styles Manage Stress

Mom: *We've got company coming. Please clean up your things in the living room.*

Daughter: *I can't. I have tons of homework that's due tomorrow.*

Mom: *You've had all weekend to do your homework! Why did you wait until the last minute?*

Daughter: *Whatever . . .*

Mom: *Don't "whatever" me. I need your help now. The house is a mess.*

Daughter: *Mom, they're YOUR friends. I don't care what the house looks like.*

Mom: *The least you could do is to help me when I really need it. Just wait till YOU want a ride to the mall!*

Our lives have become so frantic and stress-filled that it doesn't take much to tip the balance and we're overwhelmed. The

American Institute of Stress estimates that 75-90% of all medical problems are related to stress. Our physical, mental, emotional, behavioral, and spiritual health are interrelated. If one area is out of balance, there is a ripple effect to other areas. Let's face it, today's families are stressed:

- 73% of adults say they need new ways to reduce stress
- 60% of women with young children work outside the home and are stretched to balance home and family with work
- 46% of first marriages end in divorce, while 60-67% of second marriages and 74% of third marriages end in divorce.
- 33% of families experience domestic violence
- 20% of Americans have a consistent anger management problem

Brain Discovery

For every six minutes that we're in a high state of stress, it will take our immune system six hours to recover. The more we're in this state, the more our body is at risk for getting sick.

(Source: Leonard Ingram, Director of the Anger Institute of Chicago, quoted by Janie Franz in her article, "The Cost of Anger," *Imagine* Magazine, Spring 2006)

Perhaps these are the reasons why today's households are referred to as "nuclear" families—they're ready to explode.

Each thinking style has its own unique response to stress. Too much tension affects our body, thoughts, emotions, and behaviors. When strained, the weaknesses of each thinking style become exaggerated.

We have three major layers of the brain: the survival, the emotional, and the higher thinking problem-solving layers. When we become too stressed, the emotional and survival layers of the brain take over. We're so mad we literally "can't think straight." Our ability to calm down is directly linked to using our higher thinking, creative brain. (For more research on how stress impacts the brain, see the Appendix, especially Brain Facts 3, 6, 7, 8, and 9.)

Brain Discovery

Stressed families have less capacity to adapt and respect other's thinking styles. The mind downshifts from the higher thinking brain to the survival brain—a lower level of functioning—when there's too much stress.

(Source: *Human Brain and Human Learning* by Leslie Hart. New York: Longman, Inc., 1983, page 108)

We can upshift our brain to access all four Whole Brain® thinking styles by minimizing family conflicts. Observe in Round One how families can provide a secure base for learning to manage stress. Round Two describes unhealthy ways people cope when they're stressed.

Round One: *Healthy* Ways of Coping

A | Logical
- Notices and pays attention to feelings and shares them with others
- Observes body signals of shutting down or tuning out
- Listens with respect—even when holding another opinion

B | Practical
- Accepts what she/he doesn't have control over and focuses on the power she/he does have
- Becomes comfortable with change by developing a step-by-step plan to implement it
- Starts creating an environment that nurtures success—cleaning and organizing

C | Relational
- Uses a variety of self-soothing techniques to appropriately express feelings
- Clarifies the biggest concern by writing in a journal or talking with a friend
- Rather than lashing out, prioritizes what needs to be said

D | Creative

- Discovers ways to release stress without having to escape
- Finds appropriate physical ways to keep focused, like doodling
- Keeps on track by quietly moving—chewing gum or squeezing a stress ball

Adapted from the Whole Brain® model with permission from Herrmann International

Round Two: *Unhealthy* Ways of Coping

A | Logical

- Withdraws and shuts down any feelings
- Values only hearing the facts
- Becomes rigid and makes demands

B | Practical

- Remains stuck in old patterns and beliefs
- Resists making any changes
- Becomes a workaholic

C | Relational

- Intensely vents feelings and becomes more distraught
- Blames others for feeling victimized
- Wallows in feelings and won't move on

D | Creative

- Fidgets and seeks distracting activities
- Numbs out by eating, drinking, or shopping
- Escapes through fantasizing magical solutions

Adapted from the Whole Brain® model with permission from Herrmann International

Healthy parents provide a safe harbor for children by encouraging them to share all of their feelings. Depending on how the parents were raised, some may find it difficult to allow their children to share uncomfortable feelings, such as anger, sadness, fear, or disgust.

**The day the teens heard their parents say,
"We're moving out of state."**

Same Stress, Different Responses

Notice that Logicals and Relationals express their stresses in diagonally opposite ways. Logicals withdraw and shut down; Relationals release stress by venting their feelings. Unfortunately, when Relationals communicate loudly, Logicals clam up—which further polarizes the exchange.

In contrast, the Practicals and Creatives dance to a different beat. Whenever there's a new move, the Practicals dig their heels in to uphold the established routine. The Creatives become bored and start daydreaming about new steps. In return, the Practicals urge the Creatives to consider everyday realities, which only increases their frustration at someone "clipping their wings."

Parents with Relational thinking styles typically recognize feelings more easily. But, they're more vulnerable to being overwhelmed by them. Logical thinking style parents often question the validity of research that explains why sharing feelings is valuable for relationships.

When parents are uncomfortable with handling a wide range of feelings, they limit how much their children will share that particular emotion with them. Uncomfortable feelings such as being mad, sad, or fearful are often dismissed by parents as being inappropriate. Over time, children will begin expressing their feelings *indirectly, rather than openly.* Listed below are tips to increase your comfort level with communicating feelings.

How Do I Know What I'm Feeling?

One of the biggest obstacles to handling stress is to know what we're feeling. To understand the *core of your emotions,* ask yourself these questions:

- What am I experiencing right now?
- What are my bodily sensations?
- What am I feeling emotionally?
- What's "under" that feeling?
  What am I thinking?
  How are my thoughts affecting what I'm experiencing?
  What are my options?
  Which choice(s) will I make that is most appropriate for the situation?

Feelings are often revealed like layers of an onion until you reach the core. Notice the layers:
- *Anger* is typically the first feeling that surfaces, but it's only the outer skin.
- *Sadness* often lurks under the anger. Ask yourself if you're feeling disappointed or longing for something more in your life.
- *Fear* that your needs won't be met is usually near the bottom layer.
- *Guilt* or *regret* over what you've done, or not done, also influences your feelings.

Resisting feelings keeps you stuck in them. Think of the Chinese Finger Trap game. The trap is a hollow cylindrical tube open at both ends, made from woven strips of bamboo. Imagine inserting your index finger from each hand inside the opposite ends of the tube, and then pulling. The more you pull to get your fingers out, the more the strands of bamboo tighten.

So what's the secret of getting out of the trap? *Relax, rather than resist!* The key to releasing your fingers is to do the opposite of what you're naturally inclined to do. Push your fingers even deeper into the bamboo trap in order to create a relaxed space and loosen its grip. Do the equivalent with your feelings.

Five Lessons About Feelings

1. *Stop struggling when you're feeling stuck.* You're making things worse.
2. *Pause and think.* Is repeating the same response more forcefully going to help?
3. *Relax and accept what is.* Facing the issue opens up new possibilities.
4. *Recognize what you have control over and what you don't.* Make a choice that supports you.
5. *Release and let go of old feelings.* Move on with your life, rather than remain a victim.

Strengthen Emotional Intelligence

Emotional intelligence is a recently coined term by Daniel Goleman, Ph.D., to describe a set of skills. Parents can enhance their children's social and emotional intelligence by practicing these five skills:

- *Self-awareness:* accurately assess personal strengths and weaknesses
- *Self-management:* express feelings in appropriate ways
- *Motivation:* inspire others to reach goals based on core values

- *Social awareness:* develop rapport with a broad diversity of people
- *Social skills:* interact respectfully and smoothly with others

Each style emphasizes at least one of these skills. Together, they form a Whole Brain® model for increasing social and emotional intelligence.

Social and Emotional Intelligence Skills

A │ **Logical**	**D** │ **Creative**
Self-aware • Performs accurate self-assessments • Observes and describes feelings precisely • Sets goals to address weaknesses	*Self-motivated and inspires others* • Discovers each person's core values • Asks questions to understand motives • Adapts style as needed to motivate others
B │ **Practical**	**C** │ **Relational**
Self-manages • Pays attention to physical warnings of stress • Practices calming strategies routinely • Reinforces habits that promote self-discipline	*Socially aware and skillful* • Seeks to fully understand before responding • Expresses empathy and support • Negotiates conflicts with others smoothly

Adapted from the Whole Brain® model with permission from Herrmann International

Stress Management Class

Tips to Strengthen Emotional Intelligence

When parents have learned to accept and manage their own feelings in appropriate ways, they're able to teach these skills to their children. Parents using a Whole Brain® approach apply the following tips:

- Stay close to children and use *"time-in"* even when the feelings are uncomfortable.
- *Help child manage feelings* by naming, describing, and accepting them without becoming too distressed by them.
- *Express delight* in children and what they're doing when they're behaving appropriately.
- *Protect children* from getting hurt, while also *encouraging* them to explore new sights, sounds, and objects.
- Build rapport with children by *mirroring their same level of intensity* in voice, facial expressions, and gestures.
- Respond to children's needs in a *calm and kind way.*
- *Take charge when necessary* to help children handle difficult feelings in a safe and secure way.

- Accept that the *responsibilities of parenting* are to be bigger, stronger, wiser, and kinder than your children.
- *Practice daily repair moves* to maintain, as well as mend, broken relationships. Find additional resources to help if needed.
- *Expand your circle of support* to avoid making children your major source of emotional comfort.

Calming Responses for Each Thinking Style

The brain learns best when it's not under pressure. Similar to practicing a fire drill, the time to develop more ease with calming strategies is *when we're relaxed,* not stressed.

Calming Techniques for Your Family

Area affected	Symptoms	Soothing tips for each thinking style
Body	• Problems sleeping or eating; becomes sick more often due to a depressed immune system	• **A	Logical:** Set a goal of daily exercise. • **B	Practical:** Clean and straighten rooms to create an orderly environment. • **C	Relational:** Give or receive a massage. • **D	Creative:** Use art and crafts to focus energy.
Additional *physically calming strategies* for all thinking styles		• *Release muscle tension* by wiggling fingers and toes; tense and release arm and leg muscles; pretend you're a rag doll. • *Seek out soothing activities,* such as a taking a relaxing bath or stroking the family pet.

Calming Techniques for Your Family

Area affected	Symptoms	Soothing tips for each thinking style
Mind	• Problems with learning—especially with short-term memory; struggles to focus and concentrate	• **A | Logical:** Examine daily nutrition. Avoid junk foods and eat sufficient protein, vegetables, and fruits that nourish brain cells. • **B | Practical:** Use a timer to break learning into smaller chunks. Reward completion of a task. • **C | Relational:** Monitor self-talk to be more positive. • **D | Creative:** Reduce visual over-stimulation (minimize the use of television, videos, and computer games that foster short attention spans and passive learning).
Additional *mental relaxing strategies* for all thinking styles		• *Create visual strategies* by using your imagination to visualize a safe and nurturing place. • Engage as many senses as you can to imagine a positive outcome. *The brain doesn't distinguish between something you imagine and something you really see.*
Feelings	• Problems with increased irritability or depression	• **A | Logical:** Listen to feelings as a valuable source of information. Seek to understand. • **B | Practical:** Release "emotional trash" by writing in a journal. • **C | Relational:** Join a support group or seek out other community resources for assistance. • **D | Creative:** Use imagination to go on a relaxing journey.

Calming Techniques for Your Family

Area affected	Symptoms	Soothing tips for each thinking style
Additional *emotionally soothing strategies* for all thinking styles		• *Use auditory strategies* such as listening to music to release your feelings, or humming a song. • *Eliminate your critical voice.* Talk to yourself in a nurturing tone.
Actions	• Problems with hitting or destroying things; cries, complains, or "loses it." Lashes out inappropriately	• **A | Logical:** Set clear boundaries and consequences. • **B | Practical:** Spend quality time listening to the need that's fueling the behavior, such as being hungry, tired, or sick. • **C | Relational:** Teach yourself and family members to become more comfortable with expressing feelings in appropriate ways. • **D | Creative:** Repeat rhythmical movements to calm down, like rocking or throwing a ball.
Additional *behavioral intervention strategies* for all thinking styles		• *Step in and stop destructive behavior* by firmly saying: "I won't allow you to hurt me, yourself, or others. Let's all take a break and cool down before we continue." • *Step in and observe the situation more closely.* Help family members name their emotions and describe other ways of solving the problem.

Calming Techniques for Your Family

Area affected	Symptoms	Soothing tips for each thinking style
Spirit	• Problems with insufficient sense of purpose and passion; lacks meaning and seems discon- nected from life	• **A | Logical:** Set new goals to deepen one's spiritual life, such as writing a daily affirmation. • **B | Practical:** Set up rituals. Read inspirational literature regularly. Practice positive routines, such as giving thanks before meals or praying before bed. • **C | Relational:** Join a faith-shar- ing group, such as a Bible study or meditation group. Discuss your values. • **D | Creative:** Nurture wonder and awe by visiting a place of beauty or spending time in nature.
Additional *spiritual practices* for all thinking styles		• *Take time daily to quiet the body,* notice your thoughts and feelings and let them go. • *Reframe painful memories* of events and be willing to learn from them. • *Accept what is.* Make the best of what can't be changed.

Reminders

- Each style has a unique response and strategies for manag- ing stress. However, the more stressed we are, the less capac- ity we have for being able to adapt to another's thinking style.

- Families using Whole Brain® concepts make conscious choices to practice healthy ways of coping with stress and expressing feelings in appropriate ways.

- Parents listen to their warning signals and model using calm- ing strategies from head to toe.

Using What You've Learned

1. What helps your family members to manage stress?
   - What are the warning signals of becoming over-whelmed?
   - How will you set appropriate expectations for family members to create more balance in your lives?
2. How are you teaching your children to calm themselves?
   - What are you modeling to your children about ways of handling stress?
   - Ask each family member to choose one of the 30 soothing thinking style tips provided in this chapter and practice it for one week.
3. How do you respect feelings as sources of information?
   - How do you respond when a family member is upset with you?
   - What soothes you to calm down and listen without reacting?

Resources

Calming Ourselves in Stressful Moments: Helping Young Children and Their Caregivers Manage Stress by the Comprehensive Health Education Foundation (C.H.E.F.). Seattle: C.H.E.F., 2004. (See www.chef.org)

Living Authentically: Your Brain and Innate Giftedness by Arlene Taylor. Napa, Calif.: Realizations, Inc., 2002. (See www.arlene taylor.org)

Raising An Emotionally Intelligent Child: The Heart of Parenting by John Gottman with Joan Declaire. New York: Fireside Books, 1997. (See other books for repairing adult relationships at www.gottman.com)

Self-Calming Cards by Elizabeth Crary and Mits Katayama. Seattle: Parenting Press, 2004. (See www.ParentingPress.com)

CHAPTER EIGHT

Nurture Effective Family Communication

Parents: *What would everyone like to do for our vacation this summer?*

Teenage daughter: *I don't want to go anywhere. I just want to hang out with my friends.*

Pre-teen son: *I want to go wake-boarding and tubing.*

Mom: *I'm looking forward to relaxing by the lake and reading a book.*

Dad: *I'd like to play some golf.*

Parents: *Hmm, how are we going to work this out?*

One of the strengths of healthy families is making it a priority to have fun together. Each thinking style prefers some recreational activities more than others. Choosing an activity that's fun for the whole family can be challenging. One member's passion might be another's poison.

Review the following chart. Does it help you understand why your family members prefer different activities?

Typical Recreational Activities for Each Style

A ⎸ Logical	**D** ⎸ Creative
• Home improvement projects • Woodworking • Golf • Playing individual or competitive sports	• Arts and crafts • Photography • Playing music • Seeking adventurous or adrenalin-producing activities
B ⎸ Practical	**C** ⎸ Relational
• Collecting things • Hiking and camping • Attending spectator events—sports or cultural • Aerobic routines or exercise classes	• Discussing books with others • Meditating or praying • Joining a service or social club • Traveling

Adapted from the Whole Brain® model with permission from Herrmann International

Family Meetings:
Working Together to Have Fun

How do families choose what to do together when they have such diverse interests? In addition to using the Whole Brain® decision-making method that you learned in chapter six, they also participate in family meetings.

Appreciate mental diversity.

Tips for Family Meetings

1. Choose a regularly scheduled time to meet, preferably weekly, and a time limit—not more than an hour. (Practical, B)
2. Set the agenda and focus for the discussion. (Logical, A)
3. Keep the discussion on track and record decisions. (Practical, B)
4. Encourage everyone during the meeting to share their ideas in a respectful way. (Relational, C)
5. Ask each person to think of creative ways to resolve problems and to have fun. (Creative, D)
6. Make the meetings enjoyable by including snacks, a playful activity, and an icebreaker, such as sharing family appreciations or a high point from the week. (Creative and Relational, D and C)

Here's how the family in the opening dialogue applied these skills during a meeting to plan their summer vacation.

A | Logical contributions

The parents informed their children how much money they had saved to spend on their vacation. There was enough money to rent a cabin by a lake for one week that was only one hour from home. Since they weren't spending much money on travel, they had extra money left over for special activities.

C | Relational contributions

Family members wrote down their top two interests and shared why these were important to them. Everyone took turns listening. No one was allowed to interrupt or criticize what others wanted to do. Every family member's contributions were respected.

D | Creative contributions

After considering many possibilities, the family mapped out a general plan for the week. They chose a cabin on a lakeside resort with ski-boat rentals and a nearby golf course. Since the cabin was within driving distance of the teenage daughter's friends, they were invited to join her for the day or overnight. Mom would bring her favorite lounge chair and books to read by the lake.

B | Practical contributions

They picked a week in August to give enough notice at work and to make the necessary reservations and invitations. Everyone contributed ideas to the "To Do" list and took turns picking which task they'd organize for the family trip. Each family member chose one day of the week to be the special day to do whatever he or she most wanted. They were all on their own for breakfasts and lunches because the afternoons and evenings were reserved for large group and family activities.

Families using Whole Brain® methods appreciate that each thinking style contributes a valuable perspective to events. Whether it be complicated, like planning a vacation, or simple, like cooking a meal, each style approaches the task in unique ways.

Cooking a Meal The Whole Brain® Way

A | Logical	D | Creative
• Buys food that's on sale • Precisely measures all of the ingredients • Uses new kitchen gadgets	• Enjoys tasting new foods and recipes • Substitutes missing ingredients as needed • Artistically arranges the food and place settings to be visually attractive
B | Practical	**C | Relational**
• Prefers using tried and true recipes • Makes sure necessary ingredients are available • Follows recipes exactly, step-by-step	• Adjusts menu to respect individual tastes • Includes others to help prepare the meal • Invites others to join a potluck

Adapted from the Whole Brain® model with permission from Herrmann International

As you might imagine, the Creative and Practical cooks can easily aggravate each other in the kitchen. Practical cooks don't like to deviate from established recipes. Creative cooks think it's boring to use the same recipe over and over again.

Keeping the peace requires all Whole Brain® thinking styles to adjust their expectations and adapt as needed. There isn't necessarily a "right" or "wrong" way to cook—just a preferred way. *Adapting to necessary changes is easier when family members don't take style differences personally.*

Family Decisions: Negotiable and Nonnegotiable Rules

Many family arguments are about issues of power and control. Who gets to decide what? Some decisions will be made exclusively by the parents. Others will include the entire family. In a family using the Whole Brain® approach there is respect for a variety of decision-making styles. *Parents balance structure with flexibility.* They prioritize which family rules will remain firm and nonnegotiable and which ones can be more flexible depending on the situation. Nonnegotiable rules are family rules that don't change due to circumstances. Typically, parents who favor the left brain (Logical and Practical thinking styles, A and B) have more nonnegotiable rules. They prefer to run a tight ship with clear guidance of what is acceptable or unacceptable behavior.

Negotiable rules allow for greater flexibility and depend on the situation for how they will be applied. There's a greater tolerance for ambiguity. Generally, right brain thinkers (Relational and Creative thinking styles, C and D) prefer using more negotiable rules. What left brain parents might consider as back talk, right brain parents view as a democratic style of negotiating within the family.

The challenge is to be clear with children which issues are nonnegotiable and which ones have flexibility. Logical and Practical parents can try loosening up their expectations to adapt to specific circumstances. Relational and Creative parents may need to practice staying firm on issues of safety and respect.

In the illustration on page 111, the parents and grandparents express conflicting expectations about how to respond to a child who doesn't want to go to school. Logical and Practical parents prefer to take quick action to solve the problem. Creative and Relational parents spend more time considering other possibilities.

In *Growing Up Again,* Jean Illsley Clarke and Connie Dawson list the categories for nonnegotiable and negotiable rules. Listed below are illustrations for each category.

Families worry when kids don't want to go to school.

Nonnegotiable rules, emphasized by the **Logical** and **Practical** thinking styles:

- *Health:* "You may not go to school (or child care) if your temperature is over 100 degrees."
- *Safety:* "Wear your seat belt at all times."
- *Legal:* "You're underage, I won't buy you alcohol."
- *Ethics:* "Tell me the whole truth about everything."

Negotiable areas, emphasized by the **Creative** and **Relational** thinking styles:

- *Money:* "Here's how much we have to spend on school clothes. If you want brand names, you can pay the difference. I'll help you find ways to earn the additional money."
- *Homework:* "Do you want to take a break after school or start on your homework now?"
- *Chores:* "Everyone helps with chores, but we'll decide together who'll do what and when."
- *Developmental level:* "When you demonstrate responsibility, you can go to the mall by yourself."
- *Skill level:* "When you can show me you know how to safely cross the street, you can let go of my hand and do it yourself."

Different Views of Rules

Topic	Nonnegotiable Rules	Negotiable Rules
Family traditions	• "We're all going to Grandma's for our traditional turkey dinner."	• "If you don't want to eat meat at Thanksgiving, please prepare a veggie dish to bring."
Parental preference	• "When you're listening to music in the living room, please put on head phones when I'm home."	• "We like different types of music. Let's take turns with whose music is on in the living room."
Community customs	• "Please wear a shirt with sleeves to school. A tank top doesn't comply with your school's dress code."	• "You can decide which color of shirt you want to wear to school."
Manners	• "Always say thank you when you receive a gift."	• "Do you want to write a thank you note to Aunt Jane or do you want to call her to thank her for the gift?"
Religion	• "Until you leave home you'll go to church with our family."	• "I'd like you to go to church with us. Do you prefer the early or late service?"
Convenience requests	• "I need you to babysit your brother tonight. I'll pay you to watch him for me."	• "I need you to babysit your brother this evening. Would you like to take him to your soccer game or would you like to rent a movie to watch at home with him?"

Certain issues have both negotiable and nonnegotiable dimensions. Different thinking styles emphasize providing children with specific guidance or giving them more freedom to discover things on their own. Review each topic in the chart on page 112 and notice two approaches to the same situation.

Many families squabble over the grey areas of what's negotiable. Generally, parents with thinking styles in the left hemisphere (Logical and Practical) want to exert more influence over their children's lives. Taken to the extreme, they can become too controlling. Parents who are more right brain (Relational and Creative) allow children to have more freedom to make their own choices. These parents' weakness may be not setting clear enough boundaries. Let's explore how each thinking style views family rules.

SITUATION: Family rule making

Round One: *Respectful* Dialogue

A | Logical Parent
- Parents are the ultimate authority
- Certain family rules are nonnegotiable
- Gather the facts

B | Practical Parent
- Parents set up family routines
- Decisions are to be made in a timely manner
- Follow through on what you say

C | Relational Parent
- Parents set up family routines
- Decisions are made by consensus
- Everyone's needs are respected

D | Creative Parent
- Parents need to be flexible
- Certain family rules are negotiable
- Explore other options

Adapted from the Whole Brain® model with permission from Herrmann International

Round Two: *Disrespectful* Dialogue

A | Logical Parent
- "It's my way or hit the highway."
- "Because I said so."
- "I have all of the facts, what's there to discuss?"

B | Practical Parent
- "We've always done it this way."
- "We have to decide this immediately."
- "We must stick to our plan, no matter what."

C | Relational Parent
- "We can't decide because not everyone's here."
- "Everyone has to like the decision."
- "I can't stand it when we don't all agree."

D | Creative Parent
- "Don't make a big deal of it."
- "Why are you getting so uptight about this?"
- "Rules are meant to be broken; why bother making them?"

Adapted from the Whole Brain® model with permission from Herrmann International

Prioritize Your Values and Choose Your Battles Wisely

Adults and children have competing priorities. The parent's job is to keep children safe, healthy, and to instill values until children are mature enough to make their own decisions. The children's role is to push for independence and the ability to choose what they want to do.

Parents, consider yielding on issues that you'll probably lose. Are you going to force-feed your child to eat all of her peas? Is it worth it to waste your emotional energy over how your teenager wears his hair? Save your energy for more important issues, such as personal safety.

Know When to Hold, Fold, Walk Away or . . .

This phrase from Kenny Rogers's song "The Gambler" offers wise parenting advice. Depending on the situation, certain parenting responses are more appropriate than others. Each thinking style emphasizes a specific choice.

Hold firm on issues of safety and respect, a Logical parent's strength: parents are in charge of the family, not children. If you've noticed children usurping adult authority and running the household, it's time to reclaim your power as the parent. Adults must *"hold" firm on enforcing the nonnegotiable family rules.* Even though your toddler doesn't like to sit in her car seat, safety comes first. Your teens may think they're old enough to no longer need a curfew, but responsible parents need to know what their kids are doing, whom they're with, and how to contact them at all times.

Fold on issues that aren't a top priority, a Practical parent's strength: be realistic by not giving the same level of priority to all behaviors. Decide with your partner, or your co-parent, if you're separated or divorced, what's most important. To prevent children from rebelling or running away, adults also need to know when to *"fold" and be willing to compromise on issues that are negotiable.* Your daughter's messy room might be annoying, but if it's not interfering with other activities, let it go.

Walk away when you need a break, a Creative parent's strength: when parents and children are too upset to continue respectfully discussing an issue, it's time for everyone to take a break. This doesn't mean that you ignore the topic. It just needs to be tabled until a later time. *To "walk away" means waiting until everyone's cooled down enough to discuss it.* Commit to finishing the discussion at another time.

Nurture yourself—don't run—when you are stressed, the Relational parent's strength. Sometimes parents take Kenny Rogers's last phrase "a time to run . . ." too seriously and abandon their responsibilities as parents. Find additional parenting resources and a network of support. Rather than giving a child a time-out, try a "time-in." Sit with your child on the couch and hold each other until you're both calm. Or, take your teen to the coffee shop and just visit with each other over a cup of hot chocolate.

When parents model being willing to listen, compromise, and negotiate, they're teaching their children how to respect a variety of opinions. They're laying the foundation for how to appreciate mental diversity.

Reminders

- Healthy families enjoy spending time together and create opportunities for fun that respect everyone's styles.
- Families honor a variety of decision-making styles. They balance negotiable and nonnegotiable rules.
- Parents prioritize their values and wisely choose their battles of knowing when to hold firm, fold on negotiable issues, walk away and take breaks when necessary, and nurture with a "time-in" rather than a time-out.

Using What You've Learned

1. Hold a family meeting to plan an activity.
   - Discuss what you'd like to do for fun.
   - How will you decide what you'll do?
   - If everyone doesn't agree, how will you respect individual differences?
2. Discuss your family's negotiable and nonnegotiable rules.
   - How will you work it out with the other parent when one of you disagrees about whether the issue is negotiable or nonnegotiable?
   - Re-examine your current expectations. Are they realistic? If not, adjust them as needed.
   - Help your children learn how to transition to other environments that have different rules and expectations.

3. Chose your conflicts wisely.
- Review recent family arguments. Could they have been avoided? Were they important enough to hold firm and deal with the emotional consequences?
- Do you know when to hold, fold, walk away, or nurture? Or, do you limit your responses by always holding firm or regularly giving in?
- Find ways to balance your parenting responses.

Resources

Growing Up Again by Jean Illsley Clarke and Connie Dawson. Center City, Minn.: Hazelden, 1998.

Nonviolent Communication: A Language of Compassion by Marshall B. Rosenberg, Ph.D. Encinitas, Calif.: PuddleDancer Press, 2002.

Unplugging Power Struggles: Resolving Emotional Battles with Your Kids, Ages 2-10 by Jan Faull. Seattle: Parenting Press, 1999.

CHAPTER NINE

Celebrate Diversity

Son: *How come our family doesn't celebrate Christmas like my friends do?*
Dad: *We don't have their same beliefs.*
Son: *Everyone at school is talking about getting a tree and we don't have one.*
Dad: *We do other things to celebrate special days.*
Son: *It's not fair! I want our family to have a tree.*
Dad: *It's hard to be different, isn't it?*

Children learn from their parents how to handle being different and not always fitting in with others. To be successful in today's world, children need to know how to accept and communicate with a wide mix of people, cultures, and preferences. It's no longer just a politically correct nicety, but an economic necessity.

Families Model Appreciating Mental Diversity

In the past, teaching children about diversity was like reading about an exotic adventure—interesting to hear about, but not something you'd actually ever encounter. International travel and the Internet have shrunk our world. Today's classrooms in large cities often have students representing dozens of languages and ethnic backgrounds.

Respecting differences is more than honoring all skin colors or one's cultural heritage. It is also about honoring that others think in contrasting ways. Throughout history, we've struggled to accept people who seemed different from us. Most conflicts have their roots in people being uncomfortable with racial, economic, political, sexual, or religious differences.

Family life provides ongoing opportunities to learn how to not only tolerate differences, but to celebrate them.

Five Steps to Respecting Mental Diversity

1. *Recognize that fears become barriers to accepting differences in others.*

   We fear what we don't know. There are several reactions to fear. We can "fight or flee" by defending ourselves or escaping from the situation. Or, we can choose to face and embrace our fears.

2. *Accept the discomfort of uncertainty while exploring new possibilities.*

   It's uncomfortable to live with ambiguity. We prefer to have clear answers—right or wrong. Our willingness to tolerate not knowing and living with the question(s) requires great courage.

3. *Develop a spirit of inquiry—open to wondering.*

   When we pry open our closed minds and begin to wonder, we unlock future possibilities. Change won't come if we remain stuck in old behaviors or continue "preaching to the choir." It requires both commitment and humility to work at understanding another's point of view.

4. *Move from a grudging tolerance to deeper levels of acceptance.*

   Becoming tolerant is a first step towards acceptance. It opens the door to respecting others. The more time we spend with people who think differently than we do, the easier it becomes to see what we have in common, rather than what separates us.

5. *Integrate and celebrate differences.*

Beliefs and attitudes change first before there's a change in behavior. Be patient with yourself and others while you're trying on a new way of thinking and acting. Balance respecting others' needs and worldview while still honoring your own.

Applying the Five Steps of Respect

One of the ongoing arguments in my family is about time management. I like to plan things in advance and organize my day with specific details. I struggle to adapt to changes in the plan. (Notice my Practical thinking style showing?) My husband and son are much stronger in the diagonally opposite quadrant and prefer to be spontaneous and go with the flow. (Recognize their Creative styles?) As you can imagine, respecting these conflicting preferences hasn't been easy.

Brain Discovery

Accepting each others' styles on a deeper level reduces family arguments.

(Source: *Mind Waves: How to Use Less Brain Energy to Avoid Burnouts and Better Connect With Those Around You* by Arlene Taylor. Siloam Springs, Ark.: The Concerned Group, Inc., 2003, pages. 83-85)

1. *Recognize what fuels your fears.*

I grew up in a family that lived by the clock. Mealtimes were promptly served at the expected hour, with few deviations. Every week my mother required me to write out a "To Do" list and to complete a schedule listing all of my activities. I grew up with structure and predictability. When I first had children, I thought being a good parent meant having consistent routines. Although children do need stability and structure, I used my childhood experiences to justify a more rigid schedule to my husband. When he'd request more flexibility, I quickly found parenting resources that defended my point of view.

2. *Accept the discomfort of uncertainty.*
Every time I'd compromise and agree to change the plans we'd made, I felt unsettled. It seemed like a rug of security was being pulled out from under my feet. I didn't know what to count on because one plan hinged on another. Changing one created a domino effect. Of course, neither my husband nor my children anticipated the consequences of these changes. But, I could. I felt uneasy.

3. *Develop a spirit of inquiry.*
I started to wonder if others needed as much organizational structure in their life as I did. Although my husband rarely plans out his day or his week, he gets the necessary things done. He doesn't get upset by the small things in life that continually disrupt daily schedules, like I do. Could I learn to be more flexible and spontaneous?

4. *Move from a grudging tolerance to deeper levels of acceptance.*
In the beginning, I was barely tolerant of my husband and son's time management style. I would criticize my son for being such a procrastinator, such as staying up late the night before to finish big school projects. Much to my dismay, not only did he complete them, but he received good grades. I began to accept that even though his style wouldn't work for me, he was successful in school. As long as things got done, I began to relax about how he organized his time.

5. *Integrate and celebrate differences.*
When I started becoming more accepting of others' thinking styles, I felt judgmental and critical of mine. Why couldn't I be more relaxed and flexible about time? Now, I've come to realize that I can appreciate how others manage their time, and also accept what works for me. I regularly maintain a family calendar on the kitchen wall. It has an individual column for each family member that tracks appointments and activities.

My husband has learned to consult the family calendar when scheduling his work. My children know that if they wait until the last minute to ask me to take them somewhere,

I may not be available. They live with the natural consequences of not asking earlier. I mark time for dates with my husband on the calendar, but I've learned to be more flexible about the specifics of what we'll do until the day, or hour, arrives. I continue to plan my daily "To Do" list and weekly schedule, but I don't expect others to behave like I do. We're learning from each other. I've even become more adaptable at work with numerous changes in my teaching assignments. My children have also learned to plan more in advance because they want to use the car. Learning to celebrate diversity in small matters creates the foundation for managing differences when the stakes are higher.

Strengthen Underdeveloped Styles

Although people don't change their dominant thinking styles, with practice they can strengthen their least preferred ones. As in the previous example, I've learned to become more comfortable with spontaneous family activities. It has required a change in my attitude to want to develop an ease with the other styles.

Choose simple activities each day of the week to improve or reinforce a specific thinking style. Even though these exercises won't change your dominant style, they can help you to use the other thinking styles more easily when needed. For example, if you're strong in the Relational thinking style, you might need to give your Logical quadrant a tune-up by balancing your check-book or figuring out a complicated puzzle.

These exercises will expand your flexibility to think in new ways.

A | Logical

- Identify and prioritize your top two goals for the day.
- Clear out the clutter in your mind as well as in your home or office space.
- Briefly summarize what you want to say without giving lots of details.
- Learn to do something new on the computer—such as a budget-tracking program.

B | Practical

- Organize and file the papers on your desk.
- Follow all of the steps exactly when baking a lemon meringue pie.
- Make a chore chart to delegate household tasks.
- Create a family calendar to coordinate everyone's activities.

C | Relational

- Listen carefully and empathetically to better understand what others are saying.
- Create the time and space to meditate for 20 minutes.
- Write in a journal about your emotions.
- Share your thoughts and feelings with someone.

D | Creative

- Take a different route to and from school or work.
- Try a new art form, such as watercolors. Let go of creating any results and just enjoy the process.
- Pick some flowers from your garden and make an arrangement for your table.
- Rearrange your living room furniture.

Adapted from the Whole Brain® model with permission from Herrmann International

As challenging as it might be to think in another style, the root of conflicts is often an inability to value other perspectives. If you noticed muttering to yourself, "There's no way I'm gonna do that!" to any of these activities, it could be a signal that you've discovered an underdeveloped thinking style.

Appreciate Spiritual Diversity

A popular saying is: "Don't discuss politics and religion at the table." It's true that conflicting values and religious world views can create distress. Some families have a low tolerance for members who express their spirituality in ways that vary from the family norm. Yet avoiding the topic of religion isn't the answer either. We miss out on sharing our core values. Throughout this book we've focused on using a Whole Brain® approach to strengthen every dimension of family life: physical, mental, emotional, and social. Stephen Covey in his book *The 8th Habit* describes these as different aspects of intelligence. In addition, he emphasizes another dimension of life called *spiritual intelligence.*

Spirituality is the way we experience purpose and connection to something larger than ourselves. Being "spiritual" can be independent of belonging to a religious group or organization.

Cindy Wigglesworth, creator of a spiritual intelligence assessment, defines it as the "abiltity to behave with compassion and wisdom while maintaining inner and outer peace regardless of the circumstances."

Parents using the Whole Brain® model nurture their children's connection to mystery and awe. They also encourage family members to develop an inner resiliency to face whatever happens in life with a sense of meaning and purpose. Theologian Paul Tillich, Ph.D., described our era as being the "Age of Anxiety." In addition to feeling stressed by family concerns, global conflicts, and environmental catastrophes, our anxieties stem from a deeper source. Those who have an uneasy sense that their lives lack meaning or are disconnected from anything ultimate are more vulnerable to stress.

Recent brain scan studies demonstrate that those who regularly pray or meditate have greater ease in using both sides of their brain and enjoy health benefits. Prayer and meditation create new neural pathways to integrate the left and right brain hemispheres. The physiological and chemical changes include:

normalized blood pressure, decreased stress and anxiety, increased vitality, and ability to make creative connections between seemingly divergent pieces of information. Centering techniques, such as the NARN process, support all layers of the brain to act in harmony. This helps people make wise decisions.

A Whole Brain® approach to spirituality respects contrasting points of view. Moral and ethical principles are valued, as well as compassionate responses; visionary ideals are blended with practical realities.

Review the chart on page 127 to see how each style contributes to Whole Brain® spirituality.

Spiritual Parenting: Practice Forgiveness and Acceptance

Brain Discovery

"Like proper nutrition and exercise, researchers say forgiveness appears to be a behavior that a patient can learn, exercise and repeat as needed to prevent disease, and preserve health."

(Source: Robert D. Enright, University of Wisconsin psychologist, as reported by Melissa Healy in the *Spokesman Review,* January 8, 2008, pages 1 and 5)

Parents can nurture their children's spiritual intelligence by providing a wide variety of ways to express their spirituality. Choices include: reading inspired writings, participating in faith-sharing groups, taking time for quiet and reflection, or providing opportunities for social service and advocacy.

Another way of modeling spiritual values is by practicing forgiveness. Most faith traditions embrace forgiveness as a balm for the soul. New research demonstrates it is a medicine for the body as well.

Since family members know our triggers quite well, we have multiple opportunities to practice forgiveness and acceptance. Conflicts with family members often surface areas for healing. Forgiveness is what we do for ourselves. Reconcili-

Whole Brain® Spirituality

A	Logical	D	Creative
• Seeks wisdom • Wants clear principles to guide behavior • Prefers to study sacred writings • Values moral ethics • Emphasizes orthodox teachings	• Seeks truth • Wants to feel inspired • Prefers innovative approaches to feel whole • Values visionary ideals • Emphasizes eclectic teachings
B | **Practical**	**C** | **Relational**
• Seeks to do the right action • Wants to live with integrity • Prefers prescribed practices for daily living • Values how-to guidance • Emphasizes established traditions	• Seeks union with the Creator and creation • Wants a community of support • Prefers meaningful discussions • Values compassionate responses • Emphasizes personal experience

Adapted from the Whole Brain® model with permission from Herrmann International

ation requires another person to desire restoring a broken relationship. It's not always possible to reconcile, but we can forgive. Often, the most difficult person to forgive is oneself. Practicing forgiveness improves our health and well-being.

Forgiveness is another word for acceptance. We accept our humanity (and others')—our strengths and our limitations. Respecting each other's thinking styles expands our ability to affirm who we really are.

We live in a turbulent time in history where our discomfort with diversity divides not only families and congregations, but also nations. These conflicts have escalated to theologically justify "holy wars." Our human community faces increased risks if we're unable to find ways to bridge our distinctive spiritualities and world views.

As Albert Einstein said, "The problems we are causing can't be resolved in the same state of consciousness in which we created them." We're called to respect the varieties of faith as complementary facets describing the same jewel we call God or Ultimate Source of Life. Our survival as a species depends on our ability to use *our whole, creative brain to discover new ways to honor how we think, learn, communicate, relate, play, and even pray together.*

Reminders

- Children learn how to appreciate diversity by the way they're treated at home. To be successful in today's world, we all need to appreciate differences—racial, cultural, economic, political, sexual, and religious.
- Strengthen underdeveloped thinking styles with practice.
- Developing spiritual intelligence is an important dimension of life that is independent of participating in a religious organization.

Using What You've Learned

1. How do you teach your children to respect all types of diversity?
   - When children ask curious questions about differences in skin color, cultural, or religious beliefs, how will you respond?
   - If you live in a more homogeneous community, how do you intentionally expose your children to other ways of thinking and living?

2. Which Whole Brain® thinking style(s) do you avoid using?
   - How does difficulty using all four thinking styles affect you?
   - What helps you to appreciate the contributions of each thinking style?
   - Choose one activity everyday for a month to strengthen your least preferred style.
3. How do you nurture spiritual intelligence within your family?
   - What gives you meaning and purpose?
   - How do you promote a connection to mystery and awe?
   - What helps develop compassion, wisdom, and an inner resiliency?

Resources

The 8ᵗʰ Habit: From Effectiveness to Greatness by Stephen Covey. New York: Free Press, 2004. (See www.the8thhabit.com)

10 Principles of Spiritual Parenting: Nurturing Your Child's Soul by Mimi Doe with Marsha Walch. New York: HarperCollins, 1998. (See www.mimidoe.com)

The Soul of the Child: Nurturing the Divine Identity of Our Children by Michael Gurian. New York: Atria Books, 2002. (See www.michaelgurian.com)

Spiritual Intelligence: What Is It? Why Does It Matter? Why Would Business Care? by Cindy Wigglesworth. Booklet available as companion to her Spiritual Intelligence Assessment at www.consciouspursuits.com

CHAPTER NINE

Conclusion

We began this book by recognizing that each family member has a unique style of thinking. In order to reduce family arguments, we focused on how inherent biological differences shape the way we communicate, raise children, and experience the world. Families using Whole Brain® thinking respect four distinct worldviews: Logical, Practical, Relational, and Creative. *We discovered that each one contributes valuable insights in how to be a balanced parent.*

Parents learned that overdeveloped strengths become weaknesses. Exaggerated responses lead to inappropriate and unhealthy reactions. Rather than take conflicts personally, parents realized that diagonally opposite thinking styles are like oil and vinegar. They don't mix easily, and they do add great zest to a salad.

Under stress, our brain regresses to a more rigid style. Family members discovered they could unwittingly polarize each other into unhealthy positions. In a "half brain" world, discipline styles swing from one extreme to another. *But, parents using the Whole Brain® approach have learned to balance nurture with structure, as well as play and problem solving.* They appreciate that good parenting values multiple approaches. Family members can be taught in various ways to respect diversity. They can become "multilingual" and learn to quickly shift gears to communicate in others' thinking styles. Families model the Whole Brain® approach to decision making when they consider the perspectives of all four styles.

Let's review the opening dialogue from the Preface and see how Logical Dad and Relational Mom might change their approaches to their daughter's request, using the four Whole Brain® thinking styles:

Daughter: *Dad, can I go to the basketball game?*
Dad: *Have you done your homework and chores?*
Daughter: *Not yet. I'll do them when I get back.*
Dad: *Honey, you know the rule.* (Logical states the bottom line)
Daughter: *Mooomm . . . talk to Dad. All my friends are going.*
Mom: *I know you want to go.* (Relational empathetic response) *And you can, just as soon as you've finished your homework and chores.* (Mom supports the house rule and doesn't polarize her husband into being the "bad guy")
Daughter: *What if I do my homework now and finish my chores in the morning?* (Creative seeks an alternative solution)
Dad: *I'd be willing to let you go if your homework were completed before you went and you got up early to do your chores.* (Dad switches to a Relational and Practical style to negotiate the timing of when the chores are done)
Daughter: *Okay. It's a deal.*
Mom: *I know we can count on you to keep your word to us.* (Mom reinforces both the Logical style of holding firm on teaching children to be responsible and the Relational style of being flexible)

Improving family communication means understanding why different situations call for varying parental responses. Parents know how to adapt their styles as needed. For example, if the daughter does not complete her chores as promised, then her parents will apply logical consequences and be less flexible in the future until she learns to keep her word.

One way that parents can learn to shift gears to other thinking styles is by practicing the four skills of NARN: Notice, Accept, Reflect, and Nurture. They *notice* when they're over- or underreacting to a situation. They *accept* their feelings as sources of information. They *reflect* and explore other ways of responding. They find ways to *nurture* themselves and calm their emotional brain so that they can access their higher thinking creative brain.

Stressed families have a reduced ability to adapt to another's thinking style or to changes in their environment. As a result, parents make it a priority to teach family members how to successfully manage their feelings. Healthy families model responding to stress in respectful ways.

Family members strengthen underdeveloped brain quadrants. They choose specific activities to improve and reinforce being able to easily use all four brain quadrants as needed. Calming activities and brain builders integrate our ability to use our entire brain. Families spend time exploring and expanding all of their dimensions: physical, mental, emotional, social, and spiritual.

In our half brain world, more families using Whole Brain® thinking are needed! Our children will face increasing complexities and challenges. They will need to use their entire brain to make decisions. *Humankind's future is depending on it.*

Appendix

Brain Research

Parenting children can be compared to using a computer. If we're not continually updating our "software" skills, we run a greater risk of using an obsolete program. One definition of insanity is to continue doing the same thing, hoping for different results. Parenting using Whole Brain® thinking is a new approach based on research to improve family communication. "Up-grade" your understanding of brain development to enhance your family's social and emotional skills.

Fact 1: In the 1960s, Roger Sperry, Ph.D., discovered that the brain has *two major hemispheres:* right and left. A chemical bath of sex-related hormones washes over the brain of the fetus between 8 to 26 weeks' gestation. These chemicals affect boy and girl babies in distinct ways. Brain scans can identify the "maleness" and "femaleness" of the brain in a one-day-old child.

(Source: *The Minds of Boys: Saving Our Sons from Falling Behind in School and Life* by Michael Gurian and Kathy Stevens. San Francisco: Jossey-Bass, 2005, page 287)

Impact: Early brain development *influences your communication style.*

Being left or right brain dominant influences you to be more logical and practical (left brain) or more relational and creative (right brain).

Across all cultures there's statistical evidence that more men prefer the logical thinking style, while more women prefer the relational.

Michael Gurian uses the term "bridge brains" to describe boys and girls whose brains don't fit the typical gender model. One in seven females has a "male" brain, and one in five males has a "female" brain. Exceptions to the male and female brain patterns don't necessarily indicate sexual preference, but instead indicate the wide continuum of gender within the brain.

Fact 2: The corpus callosum, the great band of fibers uniting the two cerebral hemispheres, acts as a connecting bridge. Women have *30% more connecting fibers* in the corpus callosum than men, which strengthens their ability to communicate between both sides of their brain.

(Source: Why Men Don't Listen and Women Can't Read Maps by Barbara and Allan Pease. Australia/New Zealand: HarperCollins, 1999, pages 50-53)

Impact: Physiologically, *females have an easier time multitasking* than males because from birth their corpus callosum is more highly developed. *Males have an easier time focusing* on one task at a time and compartmentalizing areas of their life.

Have you noticed that a mother can be talking on the telephone, cooking dinner, and still keeping a watchful eye on her children? However, if a father is watching television with his kids, typically they have to be seriously misbehaving before he'll notice and correct them.

Women can become frustrated with men because they seem to only focus on one thing at a time. Men can teach women that there's a time to stop multitasking and prioritize what's most important.

Many women find it difficult to stop doing household tasks and play with their children. It can be uncomfortable to ignore a messy house with dishes piling up and laundry overflowing. Mothers are often distracted trying to complete all of the chores and forget to take time to relax and have fun with their children.

Fact 3: In the 1970s, Paul McLean, Ph.D., explored the three major layers of the brain and the physiological basis for why our emotions can take over and "hijack" our problem-solving brain.

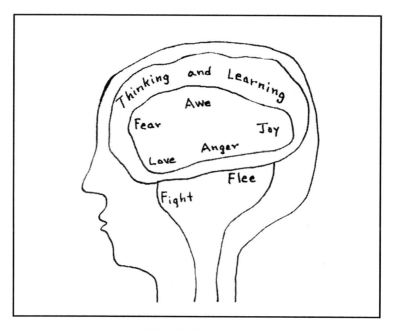

Three Brain Layers

(Source: *The Creative Brain* by Ned Herrmann. Lake Lure, N.C.: Ned Herrmann Group, 1995, page 31)

The oldest layer (in evolution terms) is the *survival* brain; it operates on instinct—freeze, fight, or flee reaction.

The middle layer, the *emotional* brain, serves as a gatekeeper between the survival and the higher thinking, creative brain.

The newest layer is the *higher thinking* brain. It is capable of thinking creatively, solving problems, and supporting our emotional intelligence.

Impact: When you're using your *survival brain,* you act first and think later. If you've ever said or done something in the heat of the moment that you later regretted, you were acting out of your survival brain.

If you notice your children "pushing your buttons," they've typically triggered a long-term memory of pleasure or pain stored in your *emotional brain.* It can become flooded with feelings and overreact.

Your ability to calm down, switch gears, and explore other options is linked to your ability to access your *higher thinking brain*. A child's ability to problem solve begins to develop about age three and continues developing until about age 25.

Fact 4: In the 1980s, Ned Herrmann developed a metaphorical description of a four-part brain that integrated the two hemispheres and the three layers to create the model for Whole Brain® thinking.

(Source: *The Creative Brain* by Ned Herrmann. Lake Lure, N.C.: Ned Herrmann Group, 1995, pages 43-73)

Impact: Parents using Whole Brain® thinking can access all parts of their brain as needed to respond appropriately to any situation. They know when to:

A | Hold firm on setting limits.

B | Create consistent routines and structures.

C | Negotiate and adapt to circumstances.

D | Use a playful approach to solve problems.

Fact 5: In the 1990s, Daniel Amen, M.D., a psychiatrist, pioneered the use of a *SPECT* (Single Photon Emission Computed Tomography) *imaging machine*. With the use of this machine, doctors can see specific areas of the brain literally light up or remain dark when thinking or doing distinct activities.

(Source: *Change Your Brain, Change Your Life* by Daniel Amen, M.D. New York: Times Books, 1998, pages 3-8)

Impact: This new technology made it easier to accurately *pinpoint the trouble spots* in the brain.

More appropriate interventions could be provided for children and adults with behavior or learning problems.

Participants received targeted "brain prescriptions," such as recommendations for medication and nutrition.

Parents were given specific physical and mental exercises to help their child behave better at home and at school.

Fact 6: Since Congress declared the 1990s as the "Decade of the Brain," our knowledge has increased more in the last 10 years than in the previous century. We've learned the brain is *like a muscle—use it or lose it!* Experience—both positive and negative —shapes which parts of the brain will be under- or overdeveloped.

(Source: www.dana.org/kids. Updated in 2006)

Impact: Brain scans show that children who've been abused or neglected *overdevelop the survival and emotional layers* of their brain. They become hypervigilant, constantly scanning their environment to maintain their safety.

Unfortunately, their problem-solving brain becomes half as developed as healthy children's because it is not used as much.

Fact 7: In contrast, children growing up in healthy environments *easily access their higher thinking and creative brain twice as much* as stressed children.

(Source: Web site and lesson plans of Bruce Perry, Ph.D. See www.childtraumacademy. com/surviving_childhood/lesson03)

Impact: Our emotions are *sources of information,* and we don't have to act on them.

More complex thinkers can sort out their options. They know how to calm down to choose an appropriate response, rather than overreact.

Children who can easily access their higher thinking brain are able to find creative solutions to problems. They can use their words, rather than their fists, to cope with bullies, for example.

Fact 8: Babies have mirror neurons that encourage them *to learn by imitating* whatever behavior they see within their environment. An infant's brain is like wet concrete. The earliest impressions have the deepest impact. Repeated patterns become hardwired as established pathways.

(Source: *Parenting from the Inside, Out* by Daniel Siegel, M.D., and Mary Hartzell. New York: Jeremy P. Tarcher, 2004, page 65)

Impact: Mirroring is *healthy when babies are surrounded by attentive parents* and caregivers. However, it's *unhealthy when children witness domestic violence* or any form of abuse.

Children don't have to have been abused to experience the impact—just seeing or hearing it is enough to cause damage. Boys who see their mother being abused are especially at risk. Seventy-five percent are more likely to have behavior problems later in life.

(Source: Fact Sheet. *Children's Advocate,* Jul.-Aug. 1997, Action Alliance for Children)

Fact 9: Skills for social and emotional intelligence that soothe the emotional layer of the brain *can be taught and enhanced.* Children learn from their parents and others how to manage their feelings.

(Source: The Talaris Institute, "The 5 Steps of Emotion Coaching," 2005. See www.talaris.org/spotlight_emotioncoaching_steps)

Impact: Parents strengthen the capacity for developing emotional intelligence when they teach their children the steps to:

1. Calm down by taking slow, deep breaths and scanning their bodies to notice their physical warning signals of becoming stressed.
2. Identify, describe, and appropriately express their emotions.
3. Access their higher thinking brain by soothing their body and emotions. Calming strategies include: singing, imagining a peaceful place, speaking positively, and using repetitive movements, such as rocking.
4. Brainstorm possible solutions and choose an appropriate response.
5. Evaluate if a solution is working. Make a plan for next time.

Fact 10: The brain has *more plasticity* than previously thought. Even though the majority of the brain's wiring is formed by age three, early (the earlier the better) and consistent intervention can shape new pathways in the brain. It's even possible for older adults to rewire their brains after a stroke.

(Source: *Rethinking the Brain: New Insights into Early Development* by Rima Shore. New York: Families and Work Institute, 2003)

Impact: It's never too late to change your brain and behavior! A Whole Brain® approach to parenting really does make a difference. Parents can *soothe and protect fragile brains* by:

• Responding to their children's needs while also taking charge when appropriate.
• Monitoring what's being modeled to their children—by adults, friends, and the media.
• Developing healthy nutrition and exercise habits that feed the brain.
• Avoiding environmental toxins—particularly smoking—that damage the brain.
• Providing ongoing love and support that encourage children to find creative solutions to problems.

You Can Teach an Older Brain New "Tricks"

Researchers once believed that it was almost impossible to rewire the brain in adults. Now they're discovering that the brain has more plasticity than previously thought.

In 2006, neurologist Nicholas Schiff, M.D., of the Weill Medical College of Cornell University in New York, documented a new breakthrough in the *Journal of Clinical Investigations.* Nerve cells that haven't died *can form new connections.*

A dramatic example is Terry Wallis, a 42-year-old man who was 19 years old when he suffered a traumatic brain injury in a truck crash. He was briefly in a coma and then in a minimally conscious state for 19 *years.* Three years ago, Wallis began speaking and moving.

Doctors at his rehabilitation center believe Wallis's recovery is linked to his family's ongoing support. His parents brought him home every week and continued to talk to him, even when they had no assurances that their son could understand them. Eventually, Wallis could grunt or blink his eyes to communicate yes or no.

Although Wallis's speech started out slow and labored, he improved everyday; now he can say whatever he wants. Sandi, his wife, and their daughter, Amber, who was born shortly before the accident, consistently provided support. Wallis says he was motivated to relearn how to walk so he could do things with his family. *New neural routes can be created in the brain when there is sufficient motivation and effort to change.* Brain plasticity is reassuring news for adults who were abused during their childhood and are committed to developing healthier responses as parents. And, it encourages people with good relationships that it's possible to strengthen them to become even better.

Families can upgrade their relationships by applying recent developments in brain research to how they talk with each other, manage stress, and teach their children.

Index